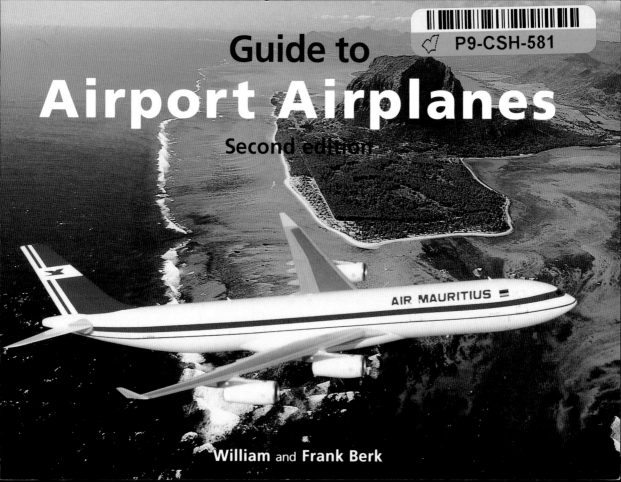

Guide to
Airport Airplanes

Second edition

AIR MAURITIUS

William and **Frank Berk**

Plymouth Press, Ltd.
42500 Five Mile Road
Plymouth, MI 48170-2544

Cover: *Boeing 747SP*
Title page: *Airbus A340-300*
Back cover left: *McDonnell Douglas DC-10-30*
Back cover right: *Saab 340*

Acknowledgments: Thanks to Bill Mellberg for incredibly resourceful help with editing. Drawing of typical modern airliner on page 4 by Keith Brown, A.I.A. Photo research by Elizabeth Howland.

All Plymouth Press books are available at a significant discount when purchased in bulk quantities for educational or promotional purposes. Special promotional editions can be formulated to fulfill specific needs. Call our marketing manager at (800) 350-1007 for further information.

Printed in Hong Kong

Contents

Typical modern airliner

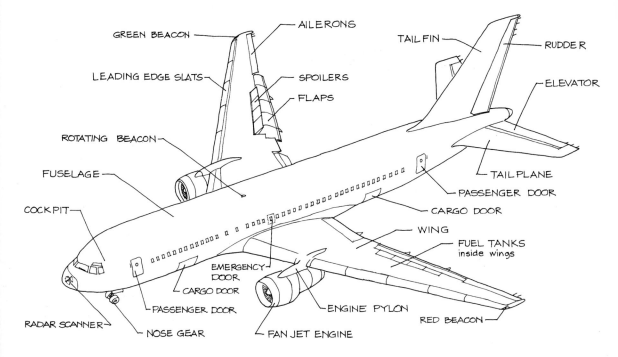

GREEN BEACON

AILERONS

TAIL FIN

RUDDER

LEADING EDGE SLATS

SPOILERS

ELEVATOR

FLAPS

ROTATING BEACON

FUSELAGE

TAIL PLANE

PASSENGER DOOR

COCKPIT

CARGO DOOR

WING

FUEL TANKS
inside wings

EMERGENCY
DOOR

CARGO DOOR

PASSENGER DOOR

ENGINE PYLON

RED BEACON

RADAR SCANNER

NOSE GEAR

FAN JET ENGINE

Introduction

Guide to Airport Airplanes facilitates identification by amateur observers of airport airplanes. Interesting information about and color photographs of virtually all airliners flown by major airlines may be found within the *Guide*. Although fun to browse, the best use of the *Guide* to identify an unknown airliner is to follow the simple self-guiding system summarized here:

1) Go to page 6. Follow the directions to find the main page number of the **GROUP** of airplanes to which your unknown airliner belongs.

2) On the main page for each group of airliners, a further division is made into **SUBGROUPS** based on simple characteristics. Page numbers of individual planes are indicated.

4) Use the distinguishing characteristics listed under the "Look-alike" entry for each airliner to tell it from other planes in its subgroup.

5) **MOST IMPORTANTLY**—have fun watching airliners!

To identify a plane, begin here:

🔆 If the plane is large with a delta wing, which is sweptback and in the shape of an isosceles triangle, with 2 of the 3 sides the same length, and looks generally like this:

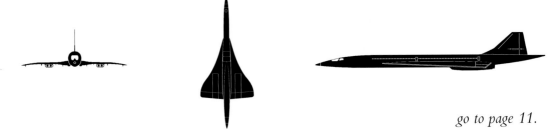

go to page 11.

🔆 If the plane has 4 jet engines, 2 on each wing, and looks generally like this:

or has 6 jet engines, 3 on each wing, and looks generally like this:

go to page 15.

❂ If the plane has 2 jet engines, 1 on each wing, and looks generally like this:

or has 3 jet engines, 1 on each wing, with the third on the tail, and looks generally like this:

go to page 35.

❂ If the plane has 2, 3, or 4 jet engines, all of which are on the tail, and looks generally like this:

or
this:

or
this:

go to page 59.

◑ If the plane has 4 propeller engines, 2 on each wing, and wings which extend from low on the fuselage, and looks generally like this:

or has wings which extend from high on the fuselage, and looks generally like this:

go to page 85.

◑ If the plane has 2 propeller engines, 1 on each wing, and wings which extend from low on the fuselage, and looks generally like this:

go to page 101.

◑ If the plane has 2 propeller engines, 1 on each wing, and wings which extend from high on the fuselage, and looks generally like this:

go to page 125.

1 **Jet airplane with a large delta wing**

If the plane is a large transport with a delta wing which is sweptback and in the shape of an isosceles triangle—with two of the three sides the same length—it must be the **Aérospatiale/ British Aerospace Concorde**, *go to page 12.*

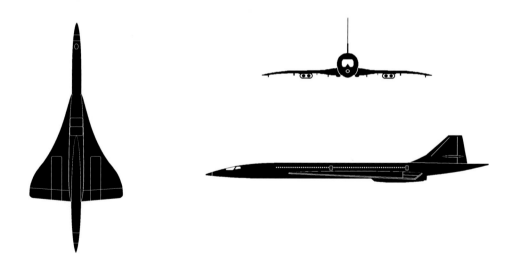

Aérospatiale/British Aerospace Concorde

Nations: France, United Kingdom
First flown: 1969
Length: 205.7 ft (62.1 m)   **Wingspan:** 83.8 ft (25.6 m)
Passenger capacity: 100
Cruising speed: 1354 mi (2166 km)/hr at altitude of 51,300 ft
  (15,635 m)
Range: 4090 mi (6544 km)
Look-alikes: Concorde is the only large delta wing airliner.

The product of an Anglo-French collaboration, planning for the Concorde began in 1962. A prototype made its first flight in 1969; commercial service was initiated in 1976. The Concorde is the world's only commercial supersonic transport, capable of travel at Mach 2 for 3900 miles. Although a technological triumph, the jetliner has not been profitable for its makers—only 20 were produced and it is flown only by British Airways and Air France.

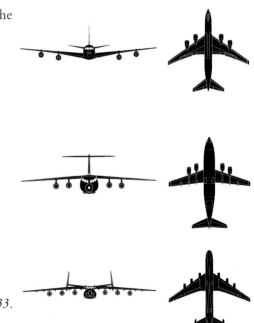

2 Jet airplanes with 4 or 6 jet engines, all on wings

If the plane looks generally like this, with 2 jet engines on each wing, and wings extending from low on the fuselage, *go to pages 16 to 25.*

> **Airbus A340**.....p. 16
> **Boeing 707**.....p. 18
> **Boeing 747**.....p. 20
> **Ilyushin IL-86/IL-96**.....p. 22
> **McDonnell Douglas DC-8**.....p. 24

If the plane looks generally like this, with 2 jet engines on each wing, and wings extending from high on the fuselage, *go to pages 26 to 31.*

> **Antonov An-124**.....p. 26
> **Avro RJ/British Aerospace 146**.....p. 28
> **Lockheed C-5 Galaxy**.....p. 30

If the plane looks generally like this, with 3 jet engines on each wing, it is the **Antonov An-225**, *go to pages 32 to 33.*

Airbus A340

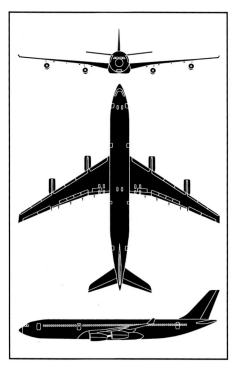

Nations: France, Germany, United Kingdom, Spain
First flown: 1991
Passenger capacity: 263–335
Cruising speed: 571 mi (914 km)/hr
Range: 9000 mi (14,400 km)
Length: 209.0 ft (63.7 m)   **Wingspan:** 197.8 ft (60.3 m)
Versions: A340-200 (longer range but less capacity than
  -300), A340-300 (heavier, longer, higher capacity than
  -200), A340-8000 (ultra long-range version of -200)
Look-alikes: The distinctive hump in the forward area of
  the fuselage housing the pilot's cabin and first class
  compartment distinguishes *Boeing 747* from A340 and all
  other very large jet planes. Airbus 340 has winglets
  extending upward from the ends of its wings, while
  Boeing 707 and *DC-8*, much smaller airliners, do not.
  Ilyushin IL-86/IL-96 have proportionately less fuselage
  behind their wings than A340.

The Airbus A340 is the largest airliner ever built in Europe, and at present is the only serious competitor to the Boeing 747 as a very large ultra long-range passenger transport. To facilitate training, maintenance, and economy in fabrication, the A340 shares a virtually identical cockpit design with the A330, with which it was developed concurrently. *Specs:* A340-300; *Silhouette:* A340-200; *Photo:* A340-300.

Boeing 707

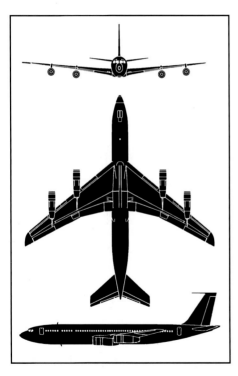

Nation: United States
First flown: 1954
Passenger capacity: 150–189
Cruising speed: 605 mi (968 km)/hr
Range: 4300 mi (6880 km)
Length: 152.8 ft (46.6 m)   **Wingspan:** 145.6 ft (44.4 m)
Versions: 707-120; 707-320 and 707-420 (stretched
   fuselage and improved engines); 720 (short range); E3A
   (electronic countermeasure); KC-135 (military tanker)
Look-alikes: Boeing 707 is very similar to *McDonnell Douglas
DC-8,* but is distinguished by having a slightly differently
shaped tailfin and in having an antenna pointing forward
from the top of the tailfin. *Boeing 747* has a distinctive hump
on the top of the front of its fuselage. *Airbus A340* is wide-
bodied and has winglets extending upward from the ends
of its wings, absent on Boeing 707. *Ilyushin IL-86/96* are
wide-bodied planes, and unlike Boeing 707, do not have
an antenna pointing forward from the top of the tailfin.

Originally conceived and developed as a midair military refuelling tanker designated KC-135, the civilian Boeing 707 was the first American-built jetliner. Commercially it was also the most successful of the first generation of long distance jets. In addition to the tanker, military versions include the electronics countermeasure E3A Sentry or AWACS, which has a large radar dome atop the fuselage. A variant was employed for American presidential transport as Air Force One until supplanted by a specially designed Boeing 747. *Specs:* 707-320; *Silhouette:* 707-320; *Photo:* 707-320s.

Boeing 747

Nation: United States
First flown: 1969
Passenger capacity: 516
Freight capacity: 264,438 lb (120,199 kg)
Cruising speed: 602 mi (963 km)/hr
Range: 7595 mi (12,150 km)
Length: 231.9 ft (70.7 m)   **Wingspan:** 195.4 ft (59.6 m)
Versions: 747–100, 747–200 (improved engines, longer range), 747–200C (passenger/cargo), 747–200F (cargo), 747SR (550 passengers, short range), 747SP (shortened fuselage, range 9625 miles [15,400km]), 747–300 (upper fuselage extended aft to accommodate 37 additional passengers), 747–400 (long-range version with extended wings and winglets which extend upward from the ends of the wings)
Look-alikes: The distinctive hump in the forward area of the fuselage housing the pilot's cabin and upper deck compartment distinguishes Boeing 747 from all other very large jet planes.

Originally conceived in 1965, the Boeing 747 was the world's first jumbo jet; it remains the largest commercial passenger transport, with many versions and continued evolution. The current production model, designated 747-400, has a range of 8406 miles (13,450 km). Special versions are used to transport the U.S. space shuttle in "piggy-back" fashion and the American president in Air Force One. *Specs:* 747-200; *Silhouette:* 747-400; *Photo:* 747-400.

Ilyushin IL-86/IL-96

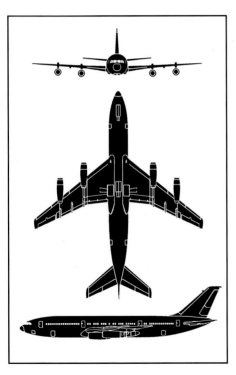

Nation: Russia

First flown: *IL-86* 1976; *IL-96* 1988

Passenger capacity: 234–350

Cruising speed: 544 mi (870 km)/hr

Range: 7190 mi (11,500 km)

Length: 209.7 ft (63.9 m)   **Wingspan:** 197.2 ft (60.1 m)

Versions: IL–86 initial version); IL–96 (updated engines and technology, addition of winglets extending upward from the ends of the wings, longer wings and shorter fuselage than IL–86), IL–96M (Pratt & Whitney engines, advanced avionics, stretched fuselage)

Look-alikes: *Boeing 747* has a distinctive hump on the top of the front of its fuselage housing the pilot's cabin and first class compartment, absent in IL–86/IL–96. IL–86/IL–96 have proportionately less fuselage behind their wings and tailfins which attach higher on the fuselage than *Airbus A340. Boeing 707* and *McDonnell Douglas DC-8* are narrow-bodied, while IL–86/IL–96 are wide-bodied.

The IL-86 is a wide-bodied airliner of intermediate range (1550 mi [2480 km]) flown by Aeroflot and other airlines of former eastern bloc countries. The IL-96 is an updated, shortened fuselage version of the IL-86, with enhanced avionics and other improvements. The IL-96M incorporates western aviation technology including Pratt & Whitney engines in an attempt to lure purchases from European and American airlines interested in a long-range (7188 mi [11,500 km]) high-capacity jetliner. *Specs:* IL-96M; *Silhouette:* IL-86; *Photo:* IL-96.

McDonnell Douglas DC-8

Nation: United States
First flown: 1958
Passenger capacity: 173–259
Freight capacity: 89,000–109,000 lb (40,400–49,600 kg)
Cruising speed: 554 mi (887 km)/hr
Range: 4500–7700 mi (7200–12,320 km)
Length: 187.3 ft (57.1 m)   **Wingspan:** 148.3 ft (45.2 m)
Versions: Series 10, Series 20 through 70 (stretched fuselages, improved engines, freighter versions)
Look-alikes: DC-8 is very similar to *Boeing 707,* but is distinguished by its differently shaped tailfin and in not having an antenna pointing forward from the top of the tailfin. *Boeing 747* has a distinctive hump on the top of the front of its fuselage. *Ilyushin IL-86/IL-96* and *Airbus A340* are wide-bodied planes, while DC-8 is narrow-bodied.

The DC-8 pioneered the jet age in the late 1950s along with the Boeing 707 and the de Havilland Comet. Production of the many versions of this successful airplane continued into the 1980s. About 70 are still in service. *Specs:* Series 60; *Silhouette:* Series 63; *Lower side view silhouette:* Series 73; *Photo:* Series 73.

Antonov An-124

Nation: Ukraine
First flown: 1982
Passenger capacity: 80 on upper deck
Freight capacity: 336,353 lb (152,196 kg) on lower deck
Cruising speed: 537 mi (859 km)/hr
Range: 10,250 mi (16,400 km)
Length: 226.6 ft (69.1 m)　　**Wingspan:** 240.4 ft (73.3 m)
Look-alikes: *Lockheed C-5* and *Avro RJ/British Aerospace 146* have tailplanes which extend from the top of the tailfin, while An-124's tailplanes extend from the fuselage. An-124 is also three times as long as *Avro RJ/British Aerospace 146*.

The An-124 had bragging rights as the largest plane in the world until the appearance of Antonov's An-225. The An-124 is very similar in layout to the Lockheed C-5, which is flown only as a military cargo jet for the U.S. Air Force. At least two western heavy lift cargo operators are flying the An-124, which has also been employed by the United Nations in relief operations. More than 30 An-124s have been built.

Avro RJ/British Aerospace 146

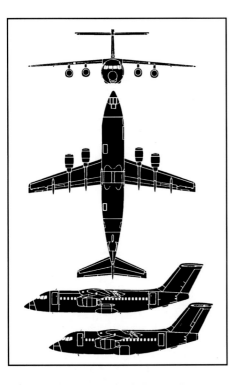

Nation: United Kingdom
First flown: 1981
Passenger capacity: 82–128
Freight capacity: 22,100–26,100 lb (10,040–11,830 kg)
Cruising speed: 477 mi (763 km)/hr
Range: 1710 mi (2730 km)
Length: 93.8 ft (28.6 m)　**Wingspan:** 86.3 ft (26.3 m)
Versions: Series 100, Series 200 and 300 (stretched
  fuselages); BAe 146-QC Convertible (passenger or
  freight); BAe 146-QT Quiet Trader (freight); Avro
  RJ70, RJ85, RJ100, RJ115 (improved versions of
  BAe 146-100, -200, and -300).
Look-alikes: Avro RJ/British Aerospace 146's relatively
  small size distinguishes it from all other much larger
  airliners and transports with four jets on their wings.

A short-haul jet, this airliner has a distinctive profile with its four jets and wings attached to the body high on the fuselage. All current production models carry the Avro RJ name, Avro having been formed as a subsidiary of British Aerospace. Over 250 are in use in North and South America, Europe, Asia, and Africa. *Specs:* Series 200; *Main silhouette:* Series 200; *Lower side view silhouette:* Series 100; *Photo:* Series 200.

Lockheed C-5 Galaxy

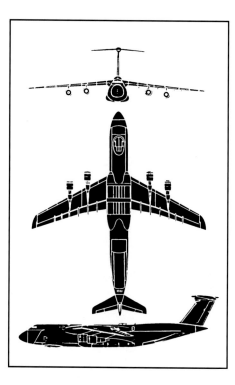

Nation: United States
First flown: 1968
Passenger capacity: 345
Freight capacity: 265,640 lb (120,199 kg)
Cruising speed: 571 mi (914 km)/hr
Range: 7600 mi (12,150 km)
Length: 247.7 ft (75.5 m)   **Wingspan:** 222.8 ft (67.9 m)
Versions: C-5A, C-5B (improved wings)
Look-alikes: *Antonov An-124* tailplanes extend from the fuselage, while C-5's extend from the top of the tailfin. C-5, although similar in form to *Avro RJ/British Aerospace 146,* is three times as long, and, unlike *Avro RJ/British Aerospace 146*, has no passenger cabin windows.

In 1965 the C-5 won out over a version of what would become the Boeing 747 as a large capacity transport for the U.S. Air Force. The largest plane in the world until the Soviet Union produced the An-124 (1982) and An-225 (1988), there are a total of 126 serving in four squadrons in the Military Airlift Command. All Galaxies have been fitted with an improved wing to increase longevity. An upward-hinged nose allows straight-in loading via a ramp.

Antonov An-225

Nation: Ukraine
First flown: 1988
Passenger capacity: 70 on upper deck
Freight capacity: 551,155 lb (250,000 kg) on lower deck
Cruising speed: 528 mi (845 km)/hr
Range: 2800 mi (4480 km)
Length: 275.5 ft (84.0 m)   **Wingspan:** 290.0 ft (88.4 m)
Look-alikes: An-225 is the only large transport with six jet engines.

Derived from the An-124, the An-225 is the world's largest airplane. Contrasting with the single tailfin of the An-124, its twin tailfins facilitate piggyback transport atop the fuselage of large loads, such as the Russia's currently mothballed space shuttle, much in the manner the Boeing 747 is utilized by NASA to transport the U.S. space shuttle. Despite its mammoth size, its interior cabin dimensions are similar to those of the An-124. Although the An-124 has found some popularity as a heavy lift commercial craft, so far only two An-225s have been built.

3 Jet airplanes with 2 jet engines on wings

I f the plane looks generally like this, with 2 jet engines, both on the wings, *go to pages 36 to 53*.

I f the plane looks generally like this, with 2 jet engines on the wings, and a third jet engine mounted on the tail, *go to pages 54 to 57*.

Airbus A300

Nations: France, Germany, United Kingdom, Spain
First flown: 1972
Passenger capacity: 247–375   **Freight:** 121,300 kg (55,000 kg)
Cruising speed: 567 mi (907 km)/hr
Range: 5080 mi (8120 km)
Length: 177.4 ft (54.1 m)   **Wingspan:** 147.3 ft (44.9 m)
Versions: A300, A300-600 (increased range), A300-600R
(greatest range)
Look-alikes: A300 differs from *Airbus A310* in having a
longer fuselage, but similar wingspan. In sideview the
bottom of the fuselage of A300 tapers upward toward the
tail from a point further forward than *Boeing 777*, which is
also considerably longer and larger. *Airbus A330* and
Tupolev Tu-204 have winglets extending upward from the
ends of the wings, absent on A300. A300 nose is shaped
differently from and fuselage extends further behind the
tailfin than on both *Boeing 767,* which is also wide-
bodied, and *Boeing 757,* which is narrow-bodied. *Airbus
A320* and *Boeing 737* are much smaller, narrow-bodied
airliners compared to A300.

The A300 was the first airliner built by Airbus, the aircraft company co-founded by aviation concerns in France, the United Kingdom, Spain, and Italy. Challenging U.S. domination by Boeing and McDonnell Douglas of the commercial jet market, their plan in 1966 to initiate production with a wide-body airframe suited for high-density continental European routes came to life with the first commercial flight by an A300 between London and Paris by Air France in 1974. *Specs:* A300-600; *Silhouette:* A300; *Photo:* A300-600R.

Airbus A310

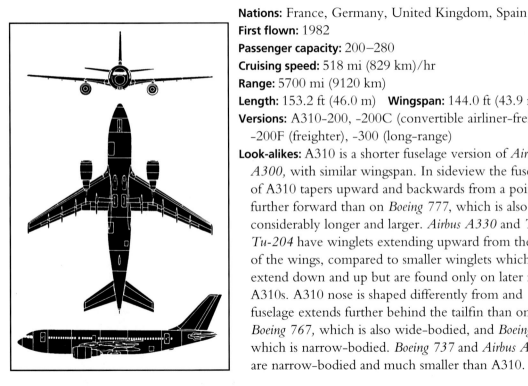

Nations: France, Germany, United Kingdom, Spain
First flown: 1982
Passenger capacity: 200–280
Cruising speed: 518 mi (829 km)/hr
Range: 5700 mi (9120 km)
Length: 153.2 ft (46.0 m)   **Wingspan:** 144.0 ft (43.9 m)
Versions: A310-200, -200C (convertible airliner-freighter), -200F (freighter), -300 (long-range)
Look-alikes: A310 is a shorter fuselage version of *Airbus A300,* with similar wingspan. In sideview the fuselage of A310 tapers upward and backwards from a point further forward than on *Boeing 777,* which is also considerably longer and larger. *Airbus A330* and *Tupolev Tu-204* have winglets extending upward from the ends of the wings, compared to smaller winglets which extend down and up but are found only on later model A310s. A310 nose is shaped differently from and fuselage extends further behind the tailfin than on both *Boeing 767,* which is also wide-bodied, and *Boeing 757,* which is narrow-bodied. *Boeing 737* and *Airbus A320* are narrow-bodied and much smaller than A310.

A shorter fuselage and lower capacity version of the A300 with an improved wing, this airliner has as its main competitor the Boeing 767, to which it is very similar in appearance. *Specs:* A310-200; *Silhouette:* A310-200; *Photo:* A310-300.

Airbus A320

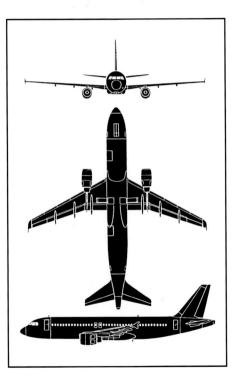

Nations: France, Germany, United Kingdom, Spain
First flown: 1987
Passenger capacity: 150–179
Cruising speed: 526 mi (842 km)/hr
Range: 3310 mi (5290 km)
Length: 123.0 ft (37.5 m)   **Wingspan:** 111.2 ft (33.9 m)
Versions: A320-100, A320-200 (greater fuel capacity and range), A319 (shortened fuselage), A321 (stretched fuselage)
Look-alikes: Narrow-bodied A320 is much shorter than wide-bodied *Airbus A300, Airbus A310, Airbus A330,* and *Boeing 767,* and narrow-bodied *Boeing 757.* The fuselage of A320 extends further behind the tailfin than on *Boeing 737, 757,* and *767. Boeing 777* is a much larger wide-bodied airliner. *Tupolev Tu-204* has winglets extending upward from the ends of the wings, compared to smaller winglets which extend down and up in A320.

The A320 was the first commercial aircraft, other than the Concorde, to employ "fly-by-wire" control, with electronic control of flaps and other control systems replacing conventional hydraulics. The A319 and A321, with, respectively, shortened and stretched fuselages, represent evolution of the original design, the A319 being the smallest offering in the Airbus jetliner series. *Specs:* A320; *Silhouette:* A320; *Photo:* A319.

Airbus A330

Nations: France, Germany, United Kingdom, Spain
First flown: 1992
Passenger capacity: 295−440
Cruising speed: 550 mi (880 km)/hr
Range: 5210−6140 mi (8340−9820 km)
Length: 209.0 ft (63.7 m)   **Wingspan:** 197.8 ft (60.3 m)
Look-alikes: Narrow-bodied *Airbus A320* is much shorter and smaller than wide-bodied A330. A330 has winglets extending upward from the ends of the wings, absent in *Airbus A300, Boeing 737, Boeing 757, Boeing 767* and *Boeing 777,* and in contrast to smaller winglets which extend both up and down but are found only on later model *Airbus A310s. Tupolev Tu-204* is narrow-bodied compared to wide-bodied A330.

The A330 is the largest twinjet in Airbus' line. Planning for the A330 and A340 began concurrently in 1987, with the four-jet A340's maiden flight preceding that of the A330 by one year. Aside from the two additional jet engines and an extra twin-wheel landing gear at the center of the A340's fuselage, the two airliners are virtually identical.

Boeing 737

Nation: United States
First flown: 1967
Passenger capacity: 115–170
Cruising speed: 576 mi (968 km)/hr
Range: 1870–3430 mi (2990–5450 km)
Length: 109.6 ft (33.4 m)   **Wingspan:** 94.8 ft (28.9 m)
Versions: 737-100, 737-200, 737-300, and 737-400 (stretched fuselages), 737-500 (longer range)
Look-alikes: Narrow-bodied Boeing 737 contrasts with wide-bodied and much larger *Airbus A300, Airbus A310, Airbus A330, Boeing 767,* and *Boeing 777.* Although narrow-bodied, *Boeing 757* is 30% longer than Boeing 737. The tail of *Airbus A320* extends further behind the tailfin than on the fuselage of Boeing 737. *Tupolev Tu-204* is 30% longer than Boeing 737 and has winglets extending upward from the ends of the wings, absent in Boeing 737.

With over 3300 produced, the Boeing 737 is the world's best selling commercial jetliner, and of Boeing's current offerings, the smallest. Although the -500 variant has a range of 3040 miles (4860 km), the 737 was originally designed as a short-haul aircraft. The current 737-300 through -500 versions are the latest in a continuing evolution which began in 1967. *Specs:* 737-300; *Silhouette:* 737-300; *Photo:* 737-400.

Boeing 757

Nation: United States
First flown: 1982
Passenger capacity: 178–239
Cruising speed: 531 mi (850 km)/hr
Range: 5300 mi (8480 km)
Length: 155.1 ft (47.3 m)   **Wingspan:** 125.0 ft (38.1 m)
Versions: 757-200, 757-200PF (freighter), 757-200M (mixed passenger and cargo)
Look-alikes: Boeing 757 is almost 30% longer than *Airbus A320* and *Boeing 737*. While Boeing 757 is narrow-bodied, *Airbus A330, Boeing 767,* and *Boeing 777* are all wide-bodied. *Airbus A300, Airbus A310,* and *Airbus A330* are wide-bodied and, compared to narrow-bodied Boeing 757, have noses which are shaped differently and fuselages which extend further behind the tailfin than on Boeing 757. *Tupolev Tu-204* has winglets extending upward from the ends of the wings, absent on Boeing 757.

The Boeing 757 was originally conceived as an evolutionary follow-on to the Boeing 727, but emerged as an almost completely new design, its wing-mounted engines in sharp contrast to the tail-mounted engines of the 727. Developed in parallel with the Boeing 767, the similarity of their flight decks allows pilots to qualify concurrently to fly both airliners. *Specs:* 757-200; *Silhouette:* 757-200; *Photo:* 757-200.

Boeing 767

Nation: United States
First flown: 1981
Passenger capacity: 216–255
Cruising speed: 531 mi (850 km)/hr
Range: 4430 mi (7090 km)
Length: 159.0 ft (48.5 m)   **Wingspan:** 156.1 ft (47.6 m)
Versions: 767-200, 767-200ER (increased range), 767-300 (stretched fuselage), 767-300ER (maximum range)
Look-alikes: *Boeing 777* is about 15% longer and has a wingspan about 25% wider than Boeing 767, making the fuselage of the 767 appear plumper than that of *Boeing 777*. *Airbus A300* and *A310* noses are shaped differently from and fuselages extend further behind the tailfin than on Boeing 767. *Airbus A330* has winglets extending upward from the ends of the wings, absent on Boeing 767. *Boeing 757* is narrow-bodied, whereas Boeing 767 is wide-bodied. In comparison to *Airbus A320* and *Boeing 737,* Boeing 767 is wide-bodied and almost 50% longer. Narrow-bodied *Tupolev Tu-204* has winglets extending upward from the ends of the wings, absent in wide-bodied Boeing 767.

B oeing 767 is a wide-bodied airliner developed concurrently with the narrow-bodied Boeing 757. With its medium-range, high-capacity performance profile, the 767 is very similar in appearance to and in direct competition with the Airbus A310. *Specs:* 767–200; *Silhouette:* 767–200; *Photo:* 767–200.

Boeing 777

Nation: United States
First flown: 1994
Passenger capacity: 305–440
Cruising speed: 565 mi (905 km)/hr
Range: 5580–6980 mi (8930–11,170 km)
Length: 209 ft (63.7 m)   **Wingspan:** 199.9 ft (60.9 m)
Look-alikes: Boeing 777 is about 15% longer and has a wingspan about 25% wider than *Boeing 767,* making the fuselage of the *Boeing 767* appear plumper than that of the 777. *Airbus A300* and *A310* have noses which taper to slimmer points and fuselages which extend further behind the tailfin than on Boeing 777. *Airbus A330* has winglets extending upward from the ends of the wings, absent in Boeing 777. *Boeing 757* is narrow-bodied, whereas Boeing 777 is wide-bodied. *Airbus A320* and *Boeing 737* are narrow-bodied, whereas Boeing 767 is wide-bodied and more than 50% longer. Narrow-bodied *Tupolev Tu-204* has winglets extending upward from the ends of the wings, absent on wide-bodied Boeing 777.

I ntended to fill a gap in Boeing's product line between the 767 and the 747, the 777 is a completely new design featuring Boeing's first use of fly-by-wire technology, extensive incorporation of composite materials, and advanced, very powerful engines. The 777 was the first two-engine airliner certified at inception for transoceanic flight when it went into service with United Airlines in May 1995.

Tupolev Tu-204

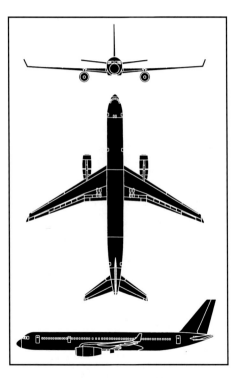

Nation: Russia
First flown: 1989
Passenger capacity: 166–214
Cruising speed: 531 mi (850 km)/hr
Range: 1810–3960 mi (2900–6330 km)
Length: 150.9 ft (46.0 m)   **Wingspan:** 137.8 ft (42.0 m)
Versions: Tu-204, Tu-204-100 and -200 (more fuel and greater range), Tu-204C (freighter), Tu-204-220
Look-alikes: *Tupolev Tu-204* has winglets extending upward from the ends of the wings, absent on *Boeing 737, Boeing 757, Boeing 767,* and *Boeing 777.* Tu-204 has winglets extending upward from the ends of the wings, compared to smaller winglets which extend both down and up in *Airbus A320.* While Tu-204 is narrow-bodied, *Airbus A300, Airbus 310,* and *Airbus A330* are all wide-bodied.

Filling a need in Russia for about 700 airliners in its class, the Tu-204 was the first Russian jetliner to be powered by western (Rolls Royce) engines. The Tu-204-220, offered with an option for western avionics, is intended to appeal to western operators, and made its first flight in 1992.

Lockheed TriStar L-1011

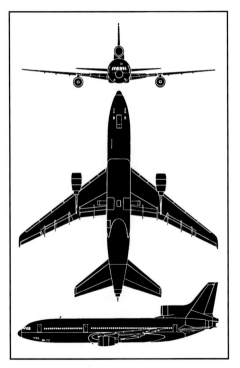

Nation: United States
First flown: 1970
Passenger capacity: 246–400
Cruising speed: 567 mi (907 km)/hr
Range: 4070 mi (6500 km)
Length: 177.8 ft (54.2 m)   **Wingspan:** 155.1 ft (47.3 m)
Versions: L-1011-1, L-1011-100, L-1011-200, L-1011-250, L-1011-500 (improved engines and in the case of the -500, a shortened fuselage to achieve longer range)
Look-alikes: TriStar L-1011 is different from *McDonnell Douglas DC-10/MD-11* in having its tail engine exhaust located below the engine's air intake on the rear of the fuselage, instead of directly behind the intake as in *McDonnell Douglas DC-10/MD-11.*

S imilar in performance and layout to its more successful competitor, the McDonnell Douglas DC-10, the L-1011 represents Lockheed's last effort to build a commercial jet transport. In addition to extensive use by airlines, the L-1011 has been adapted to tanker service by the Royal Air Force (U.K.). *Specs:* L-1011-1; *Silhouette:* L-1011-500; *Photo:* L-1011-500.

McDonnell Douglas DC-10/MD-11

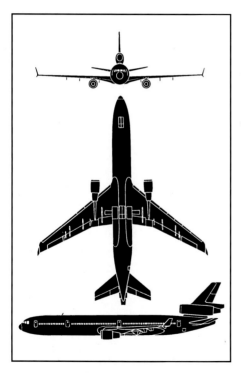

Nation: United States
First flown: *DC-10* 1970; *MD-11* 1990
Passenger capacity: 255–405
Cruising speed: 567 mi (907 km)/hr
Range: 4630–5790 mi (7410–9620 km)
Length: 182.0 ft (55.5 m)   **Wingspan:** 165.3 ft (50.4 m)
Versions: DC-10 Series 10, 30, 40 (30 and 40 have longer wings); MD-11 (stretched fuselage, addition of winglets extending upward from the ends of the wings)
Look-alikes: DC-10/MD-11 differ from *Lockheed L-1011 TriStar* in having their tail engine exhaust located directly behind the engine's air intake, whereas in *Lockheed L-1011 TriStar* the tail engine exhaust is located slightly below the engine's air intake on the rear of the fuselage.

The DC-10 and MD-11 are intermediate range jumbo jets which are very similar in appearance to Lockheed's discontinued TriStar. After halting production of the DC-10 in 1989, McDonnell Douglas' work on the modernized, stretched MD-11 resulted in an airliner which was the first entrant in the competition with Boeing and Airbus for a new 300–350 seat airliner. *Specs:* DC-10-30; *Silhouette:* MD-11; *Photo:* MD-11.

4 Jet airplanes with 2, 3, or 4 jet engines, all on tail

If the plane looks generally like this, with just 2 jet engines, 1 on each side of the rear fuselage, *go to pages 60 to 73*.

British Aerospace One-Eleven.....p. 60
Canadair Challenger/Regional Jet.....p. 62
Embraer EMB-145.....p. 64
Fokker F28/F70/F100.....p. 66
Gulfstream Aerospace Gulfstream II/III/IV.....p. 68
McDonnell Douglas DC-9/MD-80/MD-90.....p. 70
Tupolev Tu-134.....p. 72

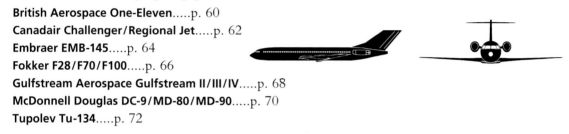

If the plane looks generally like this, with 3 jet engines, 1 on each side of the rear fuselage, and a third mounted on the tailfin, *go to pages 74 to 81*.

Boeing 727.....p. 74
Tupolev Tu-154.....p. 76
Yakovlev Yak-40.....p. 78
Yakovlev Yak-42.....p. 80

If the plane looks generally like this, with paired jet engines attached to each side of the rear fuselage, *go to pages 82 to 83*
Ilyushin IL-62.....p. 82

British Aerospace One-Eleven

Nation: United Kingdom
First flown: 1963
Passenger capacity: 89–119
Cruising speed: 541 mi (866 km)/hr
Range: 2170 mi (3460 km)
Length: 106.9 ft (32.6 m)   **Wingspan:** 93.5 ft (28.5 m)
Versions: Series 200, 300, 475 (internal improvements), 500 (stretched fuselage)
Look-alikes: *McDonnell Douglas DC-9/MD-80/MD-90* have a rear fuselage which tapers to a much slimmer point than One-Eleven. The engines on *Canadair Challenger/Regional Jet* and *Gulfstream Aerospace Gulfstream II/III/IV* are mounted higher on the fuselage than on One-Eleven. One-Eleven has a more pointed nose and tailplanes extend from slightly higher on the tailfin than on *Fokker F28/F70/F100. Tupolev Tu-134* and *Embraer EMB-145* have more pointed noses than One-Eleven.

A total of 232 One-Elevens had been built when U.K. production ended in 1982. Supplied by British Aerospace in kits, the One-Eleven is still assembled in Romania, with a total of nine having been built. Over 100 One-Elevens remain in service. *Specs:* Series 500; *Main silhouette:* Series 500; *Upper side view silhouette:* Series 400; *Photo:* Series 400.

Canadair Challenger/Regional Jet

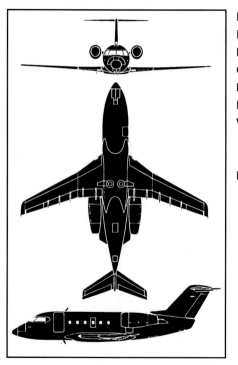

Nation: Canada
First flown: 1978
Passenger capacity: 19–50
Cruising speed: 539 mi (862 km)/hr
Range: 1630 mi (2610 km)
Length: 88.6 ft (27.0 m)   **Wingspan:** 70.2 ft (21.4 m)
Versions: Challenger 600, 601 (new engines, addition of winglets extending upward from the ends of the wings), Regional Jet (stretched fuselage)
Look-alikes: The engines on Challenger/Regional Jet are mounted higher on the fuselage than on *British Aerospace One-Eleven, Fokker F28/F70/F100, McDonnell Douglas DC-9/MD-80/MD-90,* and *Tupolev Tu-134.* Challenger/Regional Jet engines are shorter in relation to fuselage than on *Gulfstream Aerospace Gulfstream II/III/IV,* which also have a more pointed nose than Challenger/Regional Jet. *Embraer EMB-145* has a more pointed nose than Challenger/Regional Jet.

The original Challenger was designed to perform as an executive jet or commuter airliner and was the first production jetliner built in Canada. The updated Regional Jet has a larger passenger capacity and longer range. *Specs:* Regional Jet; *Silhouette:* Challenger 600; *Photo:* Regional Jet.

Embraer EMB-145

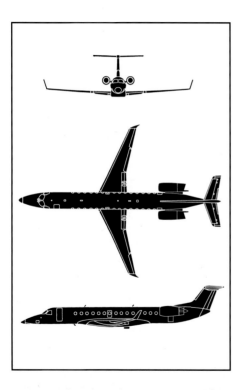

Nation: Brazil
First flown: 1995
Passenger capacity: 48–50
Cruising speed: 482 mi (771 km)/hr
Range: 930 mi (1480 km)
Length: 98.1 ft (29.9 m)   **Wingspan:** 65.8 ft (20.0 m)
Look-alikes: EMB-145 has a more pointed nose than *British Aerospace One-Eleven, Canadair Challenger/ Regional Jet, Fokker F28/F70/F100, Gulfstream Aerospace Gulfstream II/III/IV,* and *McDonnell Douglas DC-9/MD-80/MD-90. Tupolev Tu-134* is considerably longer than EMB-145.

With a program launch in 1989, the EMB-145 design is based on the EMB-120 Brasilia but features upgrading to jet from prop engines. The 50-seat regional jetliner is in competition with the Canadair Regional jet for a market of up to 450 of the type over the next ten years.

Fokker F28/F70/F100

Nation: Netherlands
First flown: *F28* 1967; *F100* 1986; *F70* 1993
Passenger capacity: *F28* 55−85; *F100* 110; *F70* 79
Cruising speed: 419−468 mi (670−748 km)/hr
Range: 1150−1770 mi (1840−2830 km)
Length: *F100* 116.8 ft (35.6 m)   **Wingspan:** 92.2 ft (28.1 m)
Versions: F28-1000 through -6000 (stretched fuselages and/
or improved wings); F100 (19 ft [5.8 m] longer than
longest F28 version with updated technology); F70
(shortened fuselage version of F100)
Look-alikes: *McDonnell Douglas DC-9/MD-80/MD-90* tail
tapers to a slimmer point and tailplane extends
considerably less further forward on fuselage than on F28/
F70/F100. *Canadair Challenger/Regional Jet* engines are
mounted higher on the fuselage than on F28/F70/F100.
Embraer EMB-145 and *Gulfstream Aerospace Gulfstream II/
III/IV* have a more pointed nose than F28/F70/F100.
British Aerospace One-Eleven and *Tupolev Tu-134* have a
more pointed nose and tailplanes extend from slightly
higher on the tailfins than on F28/F70/F100.

V ersions of this short to medium range airliner are in worldwide operation. A total of 241 F28s had been built by 1986, when it was replaced by the thoroughly modernized F100, of which over 250 have been ordered or delivered. Fokker began producing the F70, with a shortened fuselage, in 1995, marketing it as a less expensive, lower capacity alternative to the F100. *Silhouette:* F100; *Photo:* F100.

Gulfstream Aerospace Gulfstream II/III/IV

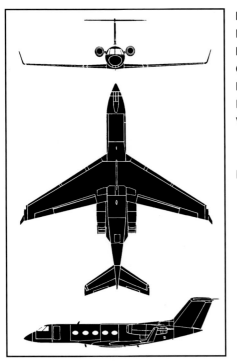

Nation: United States
First flown: 1966
Passenger capacity: 8–19
Cruising speed: 581 mi (930 km)/hr
Range: 3740 mi (5990 km)
Length: 80.0 ft (24.4 m)   **Wingspan:** 68.9 ft (21.0 m)
Versions: Gulfstream II, III (stretched fuselage, addition of winglets extending upward from the ends of the wings), IV (technologically advanced)
Look-alikes: *Canadair Challenger/Regional Jet* engines are shorter in relation to the fuselage and, like *Embraer EMB-145,* have a more pointed nose than on Gulfstream II/III/IV. Gulfstream II/III/IV has considerably shorter fuselage and fewer cabin portholes than either *Fokker F28/F70/F100, McDonnell Douglas DC-9/MD-80/MD-90* or *Tupolev Tu-134.* The engines on Gulfstream II/III/IV are mounted higher on the fuselage than on *British Aerospace One-Eleven.*

A ll versions of the Gulfstream are designed as luxury executive transports. A total of 464 IIs and IIIs were built before production ceased in 1986. The Gulfstream IV has a stretched fuselage and wing-tip winglets, as well as other improvements. Following a maiden flight in 1985, a total of 250 Gulfstream IVs have been delivered, including a version designated C-20 by the U.S. Air Force. *Specs:* Gulfstream II; *Silhouette:* Gulfstream III; *Photo:* Gulfstream II.

McDonnell Douglas DC-9/MD-80/MD-90

Nation: United States
First flown: *DC-9* 1965; *MD-80* 1979; *MD-90* 1993
Passenger capacity: *DC-9* 90–139; *MD-80* 172; *MD-90* 190
Cruising speed: 589 mi (942 km)/hr
Range: 1810 mi (2900 km)
Length: 135.5 ft (41.3 m)   **Wingspan:** 107.9 ft (32.9 m)
Versions: DC-9 Series 10, 20, 30, 40, 50 (increasing size); MD-81, -82 and -83 (stretched fuselage, improved engines), -87 (shortened fuselage, longer range), -88 (redesigned cabin, other improvements); MD-90 (stretched fuselage, improved engines)
Look-alikes: DC-9/MD-80/MD-90 tail tapers to a slimmer point and tailplane extends considerably less further forward than on *Fokker F28/F70/F100*. DC-9/MD-80/MD-90 tail tapers to a much sharper point than on *British Aerospace One-Eleven*. *Gulfstream Aerospace Gulfstream II/III/IV* and *Canadair Challenger/Regional Jet* have considerably shorter fuselages and fewer cabin portholes than DC-9/MD-80/MD-90. *Embraer EMB-145* and *Tupolev Tu-134* have more pointed noses than *DC-9/MD-80/MD-90.*

The original DC-9 was designed to accommodate 75 passengers, while the current production versions, designated MD-80 and onwards, can carry up to 187 passengers. A total of 976 DC-9's and over 1400 of the MD-80 series have been built, making them the most successful of twin jet, rear-engine commercial transports, and proving the durability of the underlying design. *Specs:* MD-80; *Silhouette:* MD-80; *Photo:* MD-80.

Tupolev Tu-134

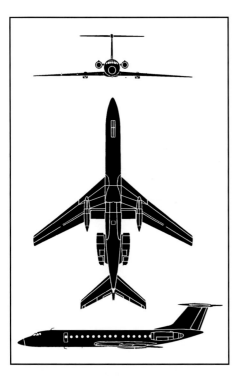

Nation: Russia
First flown: 1962
Passenger capacity: 64−80
Cruising speed: 550 mi (880 km)/hr
Range: 1880 mi (3002 km)
Length: 121.7 ft (37.1 m)   **Wingspan:** 95.1 ft (29.0 m)
Versions: Tu-134; Tu-134A (stretched fuselage);
   Tu-134B, B-1, B-3 (internal modifications)
Look-alikes: Tu-134 has a more pointed nose than
   McDonnell Douglas DC-9/MD-80/MD-90. Gulfstream
   Aerospace Gulfstream II/III/IV have a considerably shorter
   fuselage and fewer cabin portholes than Tu-134. Tu-134
   has a more pointed nose and tailplane extends from
   slightly higher on the tailfins than on *Fokker F28/F70/*
   F100. Tu-134 is considerably longer than *Embraer*
   EMB-145. The engines on *Canadair Challenger/Regional*
   Jet are mounted higher on the fuselage than on Tu-134.
   Tu-134 has a more pointed nose than *British Aerospace*
   One-Eleven.

Ashort to medium range jetliner, the Tu-134 is a scaled down version of a Soviet bomber, the Tu-16. Over 700 were built, mostly for Aeroflot, although a number were also exported to Eastern European and other Soviet allies. For many years it was the most commonly observed short-haul jetliner in the Eastern bloc. *Specs:* Tu-134A; *Silhouette:* Tu-134A; *Photo:* Tu-134A.

Boeing 727

Nation: United States
First flown: 1963
Passenger capacity: 145–189
Cruising speed: 573 mi (917 km)/hr
Range: 1670–2660 mi (2670–4260 km)
Length: 153.2 ft (46.7 m)   **Wingspan:** 107.9 ft (32.9 m)
Versions: 727-100, 727-100C (passenger/cargo with side
   loading freight door), 727-200 (stretched fuselage), 727F
   (freighter)
Look-alikes: *Tupolev Tu-154* has a forward-pointing
   antenna fairing at the top of the tailfin, absent in Boeing
   727. *Yakovlev Yak-40* is a much smaller airliner than
   Boeing 727 and does not have sweptback wings. *Yakovlev
   Yak-42* is a smaller airliner than Boeing 727, whose rear
   fuselage tapers to a much smaller point.

With 1,832 built when production line closed down in 1984, the Boeing 727 is one of the most successful commercial jet transports ever. It is also the only rear engine jetliner built by Boeing Aircraft. *Specs:* 727-200; *Main silhouette:* 727-200; *Upper side view silhouette:* 727-100; *Photo:* 727-100.

Tupolev Tu-154

Nation: Russia
First flown: 1968
Passenger capacity: 168–180
Cruising speed: 590 mi (944 km)/hr
Range: 2420–4100 mi (3880–6560 km)
Length: 157.1 ft (47.9 m)   **Wingspan:** 123.3 ft (37.6 m)
Versions: Tu-154A to M (improved avionics and engines, higher seating capacity), Tu-154C (freighter)
Look-alikes: Tu-154 is the only airliner in this subgroup with a forward-pointing antenna fairing at the top of the tailfin.

The Soviet equivalent of the Boeing 727, this airliner entered service five years after the 727. About 900 have been built, with approximately 150 still operated by airlines of former Eastern bloc countries, Cuba, and Egypt. The Tu-154 can take off from and land on rough airfields with short runways, and is still a common sight in countries whose airlines have purchased it. *Specs:* Tu-154B; *Silhouette:* Tu-154M; *Photo:* Tu-154M.

Yakovlev Yak-40

Nation: Russia
First flown: 1966
Passenger capacity: 27–32
Cruising speed: 344 mi (550 km)/hr
Range: 1130 mi (1800 km)
Length: 66.9 ft (20.4 m)   **Wingspan:** 82.0 ft (25.0 m)
Look-alikes: Yak-40 is the only airliner in this group with
  unswept wings, that is, wings which extend
  perpendicularly from the fuselage.

Of the over 1000 Yak–40s which have been built, approximately 750 serve in Aeroflot's fleet, the remainder having been exported to France, Germany, and Italy, as well as Afghanistan and former Soviet bloc countries. Its three-jet configuration facilitates operation from remote and rough airfields. In service since 1968, its basic design has undergone only minor modification, although changes to make it attractive to western airlines have been considered.

Yakovlev Yak-42

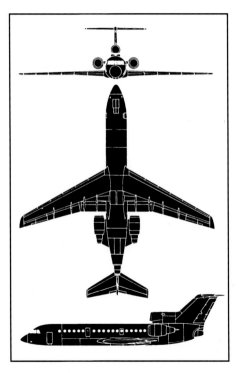

Nation: Russia
First flown: 1975
Passenger capacity: 104–168
Cruising speed: 503 mi (805 km)/hr
Range: 1250 mi (2000 km)
Length: 119.4 ft (36.4 m)   **Wingspan:** 114.5 ft (34.9 m)
Versions: Yak-42, Yak-42D (longer range), Yak-42T (freighter), Yak-142 (advanced avionics)
Look-alikes: Unlike Yak-42, *Yakovlev Yak-40* does not have sweptback wings. Tu-154 is a much longer and larger airliner than Yak-42. Yak-42 is a smaller airliner than *Boeing 727,* whose rear fuselage tapers to a much smaller point.

The Yak-42 was developed as a short-haul, medium capacity transport with the ability to operate in remote areas of the former Soviet Union with a minimum of maintenance. Its moderately sweptback wing is a design compromise between good performance on takeoff and landing, and adequate speed while cruising at altitude. Well over 100 have been built.

Ilyushin IL-62

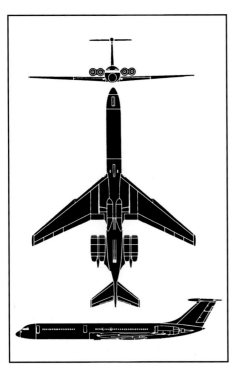

Nation: Russia
First flown: 1963
Passenger capacity: 186
Cruising speed: 575 mi (920 km)/hr
Range: 4860 mi (7770 km)
Length: 174.2 ft (53.1 m) **Wingspan:** 141.7 ft (43.2 m)
Versions: IL–62M (new engines, improved equipment,
 larger fuel capacity), IL–62MK (increased capacity)
Look-alikes: IL–62 is unique in having paired jet engines
 on either side of the rear fuselage.

The IL-62 was the Soviet Union's first long-range jetliner with intercontinental range. It entered service with Aeroflot in 1967 after a maiden flight from Moscow to Montreal. Production ceased in 1994 after 250 had been built, but the airliner remains an important part of the fleets of many former Eastern bloc nations' airlines. A specially equipped IL-62 has also served as the Russian equivalent of Air Force One. *Specs:* IL-62M; *Silhouette:* IL-62M; *Photo:* IL-62M.

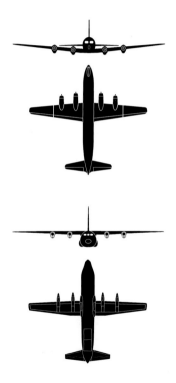

5 Propeller airplanes with 4 propeller engines on wings

I f the plane looks generally like this, with 2 engines on each wing, and the wings extending from low on the fuselage, *go to pages 86 to 93.*

I f the plane looks generally like this, with 2 engines on each wing, and the wings extending from high on the fuselage, *go to pages 94 to 99.*

Four prop engines on wings

Douglas DC-4

Nation: United States
First flown: 1942
Passenger capacity: 44–86
Cruising speed: 207 mi (331 km)/hr
Range: 2500 mi (4000 km)
Length: 93.8 ft (28.6 m)   **Wingspan:** 117.4 ft (35.8 m)
Versions: DC-4 (civil), C-54 (military)
Look-alikes: *Lockheed Electra* tailfin is shaped differently from that on DC-4. *Douglas DC-6/DC-7* have a more pointed nose than DC-4. *Vickers Viscount* tailplanes are pitched steeply upward compared to those on DC-4.

More than 200 DC-4s originated as C-54s for military use in World War II. The U.S. Air Force initiated the first regular freight service across the North Atlantic using C-54s, and one, named *Sacred Cow*, served as President Roosevelt's personal aircraft. After the war many were released to civilian service, and Douglas produced another 79 intended specifically for commercial use. About 80 remain in use worldwide.

Douglas DC-6/DC-7

Nation: United States

First flown: *DC-6* 1946; *DC-7* 1953

Passenger capacity: *DC-6* 48–102; *DC-7* 60–95

Cruising speed: *DC-6B* 315 mi (504 km)/hr
                       DC-7C 355 mi (568 km)/hr

Freight capacity: *DC-7F* 34,600 lb (15,700 kg)

Range: *DC-6B* 3010 mi (4810 km)
          DC-7C 4700 mi (7530 km)

Length: *DC-6B* 105.6 ft (32.2 m) **Wingspan:** 117.4 ft (35.8 m)

Versions: DC-6, DC-6A and B (stretched fuselage), DC-7 (further stretched fuselage), DC-7B (longer range), DC-7C (maximally stretched fuselage and extended wing), DC-7F (freighter)

Look-alikes: DC-6/DC-7 are larger than and have a nose which is more pointed than *Lockheed L-188 Electra, Douglas DC-4,* and *Vickers Viscount.*

The DC-6 has a longer fuselage and more range than the DC-4, from which it was derived. The DC-7B, a stretched version of DC-6, was designed for nonstop North Atlantic crossings. DC-7C inaugerated transpolar flights, flying between Tokyo and Copenhagen in 1957. About 100 DC-6s and 40 DC-7s remain in operation. *Main silhouette:* DC-6B; *Upper side view silhouette:* DC-6; *Photo:* DC-6B.

Lockheed L-188 Electra

Nation: United States
First flown: 1957
Passenger capacity: 66–99
Freight capacity: 26,000 lb (11,820 kg)
Cruising speed: 405 mi (648 km)/hr
Range: 2770 mi (4430 km)
Length: 104.3 ft (31.8 m)   **Wingspan:** 99.1 ft (30.2 m)
Versions: L-188A, L-188C (longer range), P-3 Orion
(anti-submarine military version)
Look-alikes: Electra tailplanes extend from higher on the
fuselage than on *Douglas DC-4, DC-6* and *DC-7. Vickers
Viscount* is smaller than Electra, and has steeply upwardly
pitched tailplanes.

In the first years of its operation the Electra suffered two disastrous crashes, eventually found to have resulted from metal fatigue. Structural modifications were made to the wings, solving the problem. The approximately 50 Electras active today are mainly flown as commercial freighters. A military derivative is the P-3 Orion anti-submarine aircraft, easily identified by the absence of cabin windows and a boom extending from the rear of the fuselage.

Vickers Viscount

Nation: United Kingdom
First flown: 1948
Passenger capacity: 47–71
Cruising speed: 357 mi (571 km)/hr
Range: 1730 mi (2760 km)
Length: 85.6 ft (26.1 m)   **Wingspan:** 93.8 ft (28.6 m)
Versions: Series 700, 700D, 770D, 800, 810 (increasing payload, stretched fuselage, cabin improvements)
Look-alikes: Viscount is smaller than *Lockheed Electra* and has more steeply upwardly pitched tailplanes. *Douglas DC-6/DC-7* are larger than and have a tailfin shaped differently from Viscount's. Viscount's tailplanes are pitched steeply upward compared to those on *Douglas DC-4.*

The world's first commercial turboprop, the Viscount is still flown in many countries both as a passenger plane and freighter. A total of 440 were built through 1964, of which more than 30 remain in service. *Specs:* 810; *Main silhouette:* 800; *Upper side view silhouette:* 700; *Photo:* 800.

Antonov An-12

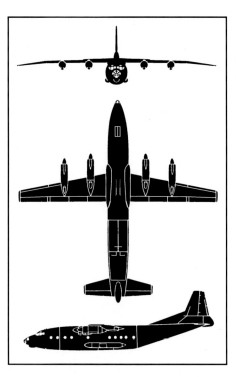

Nation: Ukraine
First flown: 1957
Passenger capacity: 84–100
Cruising speed: 419 mi (670 km)/hr
Range: 3560 mi (5700 km)
Length: 108.6 ft (33.1 m)   **Wingspan:** 124.6 ft (38.0 m)
Look-alikes: *Lockheed C-130/L-100* have a more pointed nose than An-12, and wings which do not "droop" as they extend from the fuselage. *De Havilland DHC Dash 7* has tailplanes extending from much higher on the tailfin than An-12.

A very numerous Soviet transport with over 900 produced up to 1973. Many An-12s are still active today in both military and civilian roles. Similar in appearance to the Lockheed C-130, the An-12 has been exported to many countries including the People's Republic of China, Bulgaria, Cuba, Iraq, Poland, and Guinea. China has manufactured a redesigned An-12 in cooperation with Lockheed.

de Havilland DHC-7 Dash 7

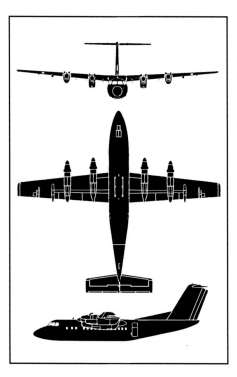

Nation: Canada
First flown: 1975
Passenger capacity: 50–54
Cruising speed: 266 mi (426 km)/hr
Range: 850 mi (1350 km)
Length: 80.4 ft (24.5 m)   **Wingspan:** 93.2 ft (28.4 m)
Versions: Series 100, Series 101 (freighter), Series 150 (increased payload), Series 151 (freighter version of Series 150)
Look-alikes: Dash 7 tailplanes extend from much higher on the tailfin than tailplanes on *Antonov An-12* and *Lockheed C-130/L-100.*

Designed for use at close-in downtown city airports, the Dash 7 is exceptionally quiet and capable of takeoff and landing from runways as short as 2000 feet, qualifying it as a "STOL"—short takeoff and landing—airliner. Total production was 111 between 1977 and 1988. *Specs:* Series 100; *Silhouette:* Series 100; *Photo:* Series 100.

Lockheed C-130 Hercules/L-100

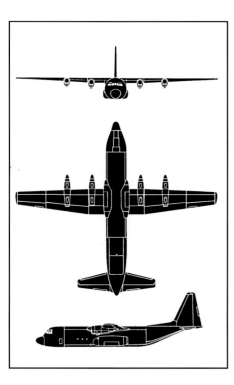

Nation: United States
First flown: 1954
Passenger capacity: 79–100
Freight capacity: 45,300 lb (20,590 kg)
Cruising speed: 355 mi (568 km)/hr
Range: 1840–5560 mi (2950–8900 km)
Length: 112.8 ft (34.4 m)   **Wingspan:** 132.5 ft (40.4 m)
Versions: Many tailored to specific tasks
Look-alikes: Lockheed C-130/L-100 has a more pointed nose than *Antonov An-12*, and wings which do not "droop" as they extend from the fuselage. *De Havilland DHC Dash 7* tailplanes extend from much higher on the tailfin than tailplanes on C-130/L-100.

One of the most numerous military transports built in the west, the C-130 has been adapted to such uses as troop transport (C-130H), tanker (C130F), gunship (AC-130E), and communications (EC-130). The L-100 is the civilian freighter version, although many military C-130s have also been converted to commercial use. *Specs:* L-100; *Silhouette:* L-100; *Photo:* C-130.

6 Propeller airplanes with 2 engines on wings; Wings extend from low on the fuselage

If the plane looks generally like this, with tailplanes extending from the fuselage, *go to pages 102 to 115.*

British Aerospace 748/ATP/Jetstream 61.....p. 102
Convair 240-640.....p. 104
Douglas DC-3.....p. 106
Embraer EMB-110 Bandeirante.....p. 108
Gulfstream Aerospace Gulfstream I/I-C.....p. 110
Ilyushin IL-114....p. 112
Saab 340/2000.....p. 114

If the plane looks generally like this, with tailplanes extending from the tailfin below its top, *go to pages 116 to 119.*

Fairchild Metro.....p. 116
Jetstream 31/41.....p. 118

If the plane looks generally like this, with tailplanes extending from the top of tailfin, *go to pages 120 to 123.*

Beechcraft 1900.....p. 120
Embraer EMB-120 Brasilia.....p. 122

British Aerospace 748/ATP/Jetstream 61

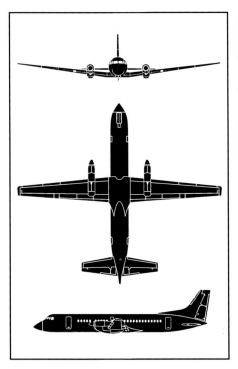

Nation: United Kingdom
First flown: *748* 1960; *ATP* 1986; *Jetstream 61* 1994
Passenger capacity: *748* 40–58; *ATP* 64–68;
                              Jetstream 61 70
Cruising speed: *748* 282 mi (451 km)/hr; *ATP* 306 mi
   (489 km)/hr; *Jetstream 61* 313 mi (500 km)/hr
Range: 738 mi (1180 km)
Length: 85.3 ft (26.0 m)   **Wingspan:** 100.4 ft (30.6 m)
Versions: 748, Super 748 (improved engines), ATP (see
   text), Jetstream 61 (see text)
Look-alikes: *Convair 240-640* and *Douglas DC-3* have
   differently shaped tailfins from 748/ATP/Jetstream 61.
   Gulfstream Aerospace Gulfstream I/I-C and *Saab 340/2000*
   tailplanes pitch upward from their fuselages, while those
   on 748/ATP/Jetstream 61 do not. *Embraer EMB-110* is
   much smaller than 748/ATP/Jetstream 61 with a very
   differently shaped fuselage. 748/ATP/Jetstream 61 tailfin
   is shaped differently from that on *Ilyushin IL-114*.

The models in this family are the largest twin prop-powered airliners now flown in the west. The 748 was designed in the 1950s as a replacement for the DC-3 and its contemporaries. A total of 381 were produced between 1961 and 1986 before the advent of the ATP, a stretched derivative with updated engines. The Jetstream 61 is identical in appearance to the ATP and represents further improvement of the engines and interior of the plane. *Specs:* Jetstream 61; *Silhouette:* ATP; *Photo:* 748.

Convair 240/340/440/540/580/600/640

Nation: United States
First flown: 1947
Passenger capacity: 44–56
Freight capacity: 15,000 lb (6818 kg)
Cruising speed: 301 mi (482 km)/hr
Range: 1230 mi (1970 km)
Length: 79.0 ft (24.1 m)   **Wingspan:** 105.3 ft (32.1 m)
Versions: Increased length of fuselage and replacement of
  piston engines with turboprops in versions 540 onwards
Look-alikes: *British Aerospace 748/ATP, Douglas DC-3,
  Gulfstream Aerospace Gulfstream I/I-C,* and *Ilyushin IL-114*
  tailfins are shaped differently from those on Convair.
  Saab 340/2000 tailplanes pitch upward from the fuselage,
  while those on Convair do not. *Embraer EMB-110* is a
  much smaller airliner and has a differently shaped
  fuselage.

Evolving over 21 years of production, early improvements on this Convair series included lengthening the fuselage. A total of 1081 of the early Convair 240s, 340s, and 440s were produced, including 99 C-131s (military version of the Convair 340). Versions numbered Convair 540 and onwards represented upgrading of older versions from piston to turboprop engines. Many are still in use as freighters. *Specs:* Convair 640; *Silhouette:* Convair 340; *Photo:* Convair 640.

Douglas DC-3

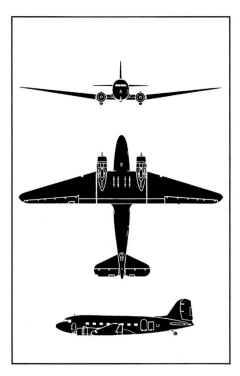

Nation: United States
First flown: 1935
Passenger capacity: 21–36
Cruising speed: 185 mi (298 km)/hr
Range: 1520 mi (2430 km)
Length: 64.6 ft (19.7 m)   **Wingspan:** 95.1 ft (29.0 m)
Versions: DC–3A and B (improved engines); many military versions including C-47; Lisunov Li-2 (produced under license in Soviet Union); L2D (under license in Japan)
Look-alikes: *British Aerospace 748/ATP/Jetstream 61* and *Convair 240-640* tailfins are shaped differently than that on DC-3. *Gulfstream I/I-C* and *Saab 340/2000* tailplanes pitch upward from the fuselage, while those on DC-3 do not. *Embraer EMB-110* is much smaller and has a very differently shaped fuselage from DC-3. *Ilyushin IL-114* tailfins and fuselage are shaped differently than those on DC-3.

Perhaps the most celebrated of all air transports, the DC–3 is also the most prolifically manufactured airliner/freighter ever — over 12,000 were built, many for service in World War II. Eisenhower called the C-47 one of the four most significant weapons in the war. Converted military models were the backbone of civilian airline fleets in the immediate postwar period. Several hundred are still in use.

Embraer EMB-110 Bandeirante

Nation: Brazil
First flown: 1968
Passenger capacity: 21
Cruising speed: 259 mi (414 km)/hr
Range: 1180 mi (1890 km)
Length: 50.2 ft (15.3 m)   **Wingspan:** 49.5 ft (15.1 m)
Versions: 12 versions adapted for specific military/civilian uses
Look-alikes: All similar looking planes except *Saab 340* are much larger than EMB-110. *Saab 340/2000* have tailplanes which pitch upward from the fuselage, while those on EMB-110 do not.

The successful first product of Embraer (Empresa Brasileira de Aeronautica), the Bandeirante—or "Bandit"—was designed in many versions for the Brazilian military. Production ceased in 1990 after a total of 500 had been produced, but the airliner remains popular with commuter airlines worldwide due to its dependability and low-cost maintenance.

Gulfstream Aerospace Gulfstream I/I-C

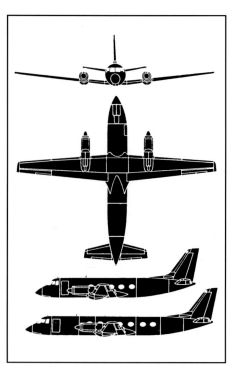

Nation: United States
First flown: 1958
Passenger capacity: 24–37
Cruising speed: 350 mi (560 km)/hr
Range: 2560 mi (4090 km)
Length: 80.0 ft (19.4 m)   **Wingspan:** 78.4 ft (23.9 m)
Versions: I, I-C (stretched fuselage)
Look-alikes: Gulfstream I/I-C and *Saab 340* tailplanes pitch upward from the fuselage, distinguishing them from airliners otherwise similar in appearance. Gulfstream I/I-C have tailplanes pitch upward less steeply from the fuselage than those on *Saab 340/2000,* as well as distinctive large, oval cabin windows.

The Gulfstream I was designed as a business plane, while the I–C was a conversion featuring extended fuselage and increased capacity, making it suitable as a commuter airliner. Originating with the Grumman American Aviation Corporation, rights for the Gulfstream were obtained by American Jet Industries in 1978, when the Grumman American subsidiary was purchased from Grumman Corporation. A total of 200 Gulfstream Is were produced, with five conversions to I–C performed. *Specs:* Gulfstream I; *Main silhouette:* Gulfstream I; *Lower side view silhouette:* Gulfstream I–C; *Photo:* Gulfstream I.

Ilyushin IL-114

Nation: Russia
First flown: 1990
Passenger capacity: 64
Cruising speed: 313 mi (500 km)/hr
Range: 3000 mi (4800 km)
Length: 88.3 ft (26.9 m)   **Wingspan:** 98.4 ft (30.0 m)
Look-alikes: *British Aerospace 748/ATP/Jetstream 61* tailfin is shaped differently from IL-114. *Douglas DC-3* tailfins and fuselage are different shapes than those on IL-114. *Convair 240-640* tailfins are shaped differently from those on IL-114. Gulfstream *Aerospace Gulfstream I/I-C* and *Saab 340/2000* tailplanes pitch upward from the fuselage, whereas tailplanes on IL-114 do not. *Embraer EMB-110* is a much smaller airliner with a fuselage shaped differently than that on IL-114.

Amodern design intended to replace aging turboprop airliners, including the Antonov An-24/26, the IL-114 was built to fulfill an Aeroflot requirement for about 500 of the type. Consideration has been given both to a stretched variant with a capacity of 75 passengers and to a westernized version which would be fitted with American-built engines. Almost 400 IL-114s have been ordered, mostly by Aeroflot and its successor airlines.

Saab 340/2000

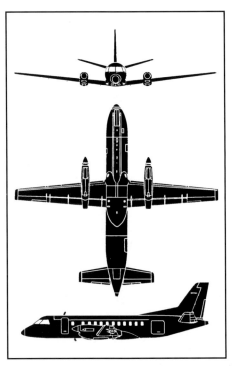

Nation: Sweden
First flown: *Saab 340* 1983; *Saab 2000* 1992
Passenger capacity: *Saab 340* 35; *Saab 2000* 50
Cruising speed: *Saab 340* 313 mi (501 km)/hr
           Saab 2000 424 mi (678 km)/hr
Range: *Saab 340* 1080 mi (1730 km)
      Saab 2000 1650 mi (2640 km)
Length: *Saab 340* 64.6 ft (19.7 m)
       Saab 2000 88.7 ft (27.0 m)
Wingspan: *Saab 340* 70.2 ft (21.4 m)
         Saab 2000 81.3 ft (24.8 m)
Versions: 340A, 340B (more powerful engines, larger
  tailplanes, extended range); 2000 (stretched fuselage,
  many other improvements)
Look-alikes: Saab 340/2000 and *Gulfstream I/I-C* tailplanes
  pitch upward from their fuselages, distinguishing them
  from other planes of similar appearance. Saab 340/2000
  tailplanes are more steeply upwardly pitched than
  Gulfstream I/I-C, which have distinctive large, oval cabin
  windows.

Originally a joint project with the U.S. firm Fairchild, the Saab 340 was taken over completely by Saab in 1987. The 2000, a stretched, higher capacity evolution of the 340, has powerful new engines which allow it to attain close to jet speed. It entered service in 1994 with Crossair of Switzerland. Over 400 Saab 340s and about 40 Saab 2000s have been sold. *Silhouette: 340A; Photo: 2000.*

Two props with wings low on fuselage

Fairchild Metro

Nation: United States
First flown: 1969
Passenger capacity: 19
Cruising speed: 288 mi (460 km)/hr
Range: 1010 mi (1610 km)
Length: 59.4 ft (18.1 m)   **Wingspan:** 57.1 ft (17.4 m)
Versions: Metro, Metro III (longer wing), Merlin IV (business), Expediter (cargo), Metro 23 (higher takeoff weight, improved engines)
Look-alikes: Metro differs from *Jetstream 31/41* in having tailplanes which extend from lower on the tailfin and which are sweptback, as well as in having a more pointed nose.

With almost 1000 built, the Metro is one of the most successful of a class of regional airliners designed to carry up to 19 passengers. This is the largest capacity plane allowed by Federal Aviation Administration regulations to be operated without a cabin attendant. The various Metro versions are almost identical in appearance. *Specs:* Metro III; *Silhouette:* Metro III; *Photo:* Metro III.

Jetstream 31/41

Nation: United Kingdom
First flown: *Jetstream 31* 1967; *Jetstream 41* 1991
Passenger capacity: *Jetstream 31* 19; *Jetstream 41* 29
Cruising speed: *Jetstream 31* 305 mi (492 km)/hr
　　　　　　　　Jetstream 41 340 mi (550 km)/hr
Range: *Jetstream 31* 748 mi (1192 km)
　　　　Jetstream 41 789 mi (1263 km)
Length: *Jetstream 31* 47.2 ft (14.4 m)
　　　　Jetstream 41 63.3 ft (19.3 m)
Wingspan: *Jetstream 31* 52.2 ft (15.9 m)
　　　　　Jetstream 41 60.3 ft (18.3 m)
Versions: 31, Super 31 (upgraded engines, improved
　performance), 41 (stretched fuselage, further improved
　performance)
Look-alikes: *Fairchild Metro* differs from Jetstream 31/41 in
　having tailplanes which extend from lower on the tailfin
　and which are sweptback, as well as in having a more
　pointed nose.

The Jetstream has a varied corporate heritage, having first been manufactured by Handley Page and then by Scottish Aviation, which was in turn absorbed by British Aerospace. The Jetstream 41, based on the 31, features a 16.0 ft (4.9 m) stretched fuselage. Both planes are now marketed by BAe's Jetstream subsidiary. Almost 400 Jetstream 31s and over 60 Jetstream 41s have been produced. *Silhouette: Jetstream 31; Photo:* Jetstream 41.

Beechcraft 1900

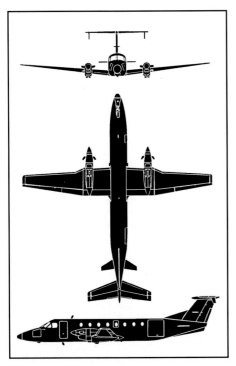

Nation: United States
First flown: 1982
Passenger capacity: 19
Cruising speed: 310 mi (496 km)/hr
Range: 1490 mi (2380 km)
Length: 57.7 ft (17.6 m)   **Wingspan:** 54.4 ft (16.6 m)
Versions: 1900C (passenger/cargo), 1900C Exec-Liner
(business), C-12J (military); 1900D (deeper fuselage
allows passengers to stand, larger passenger and freight
doors, larger windows)
Look-alikes: The tail-lets which extend down from the
tailplanes and the small horizontal tail surfaces extending
from the rear of the fuselage are unique to the Beechcraft
1900C.

I n competition with the more successful Fairchild Metro, this regional airliner can carry 19 passengers, the most allowed by Federal Aviation Administration regulations without a cabin attendant. A number of military versions are available to fulfill roles in transport, maritime patrol, and electronic surveillance. Over 340 have been built or ordered. *Specs:* 1900C; *Silhouette:* 1900C; *Photo:* 1900C.

Embraer EMB-120 Brasilia

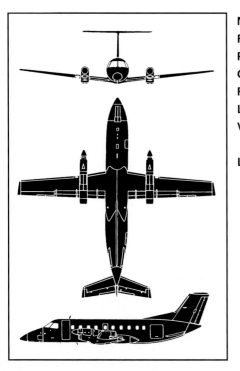

Nation: Brazil
First flown: 1983
Passenger capacity: 18–30
Cruising speed: 343 mi (549 km)/hr
Range: 1860 mi (2980 km)
Length: 65.6 ft (20.0 m)   **Wingspan:** 64.9 ft (19.8 m)
Versions: cargo and military versions for Brazilian armed forces
Look-alikes: In contrast to the *Beechcraft 1900C,* the EMB-120 lacks the distinctive tail-lets which extend down from the tailplane and the small horizontal tail surfaces extending from the rear of the fuselage.

After the success of the EMB-110 Bandeirante, Embraer embarked on development of the larger and more ambitious EMB-120. An unusual example of a commercially successful transport built by a developing country, over 300 EMB-120s are flown by airlines in both North America and Europe.

7 Propeller airplanes with 2 engines on wings; Wings extend from high on the fuselage

I f the plane looks like this, with tailplanes extending from the lower part of the tailfin or from the fuselage, *go to pages 126 to 143.*

I f the plane looks like this, with tailplanes attached at or near the top of the tailfin, *go to pages 144 to 151.*

I f the plane looks like this, with twin tailfins and a boxlike fuselage, *go to pages 150 to 153.*

Aérospatiale N 262/Fregate

Nation: France
First flown: 1962
Passenger capacity: 26 – 29
Cruising speed: 246 mi (394 km)/hr
Range: 590 mi (950 km)
Length: 63.3 ft (19.3 m)   **Wingspan:** 74.1 ft (22.6 m)
Versions: A, B, C, D (engine variations); Mohawk 298
   (new engines and updated technology for use in the U.S.)
Look-alikes: N 262, *Airtech CN-235, CASA C-212 Aviocar,
   Dornier 228, Let L 410/L 420* and *Shorts 360* are
   distinguished by landing gear pods of various shapes and
   sizes protruding from the lower part of their fuselages
   under the wings. To discern these from one another:
   Airtech CN-235 has a less pointed nose than N 262, while
   CASA C-212 Aviocar and *Dornier 228* have more pointed
   noses than N 262; *Shorts 360* has braces extending from
   the landing gear pods on the fuselage upward to the
   wings on either side; and *Let L 410/L 420* tailfin extends
   below the aft fuselage.

Of the 111 copies of this short-haul commuter which were produced, approximately 20 are flown as airliners, while some remain in service with the French Air Force. In the late 1970s, the commuter airline Allegheny Airlines initiated an extensive upgrade program for its N 262s, fitting them with upgraded engines and improved avionics. This version is known as the Mohawk 298, after the Allegheny subsidiary which flew the plane. *Specs:* N 262; *Silhouette:* N 262; *Photo:* N 262.

Airtech CN-235

Nations: Spain, Indonesia
First flown: 1983
Passenger capacity: 45
Cruising speed: 281 mi (450 km)/hr
Range: 2450 mi (3910 km)
Length: 70.2 ft (21.4 m)　**Wingspan:** 84.6 ft (25.8 m)
Versions: Series 10, Series 100 (upgraded engines)
Look-alikes: CN-235, *Aérospatiale N 262, CASA C-212 Aviocar, Dornier 228, Let L 410/L 420* and *Shorts 360* are distinguished by landing gear pods of various shapes and sizes protruding from the lower part of their fuselages under the wings. To discern these from one another: CN-235 has a less pointed nose than *Aérospatiale N 262/ Fregate, CASA C-212 Aviocar,* and *Dornier 228; Shorts 360* has braces extending from the landing gear pods on the fuselage upward to the wings on either side, while *Let L 410/L 420* tailfin extends below the aft fuselage.

A joint effort of aircraft companies based in Spain (Construcciones Aeronauticas SA) and Indonesia (I.P.T.N.), the CN-235 was designed for both military and civilian use. Although each nation takes responsibility for fabricating specific components, final assembly takes place in both countries. Over 200 have been produced.

Antonov An-24/An-26

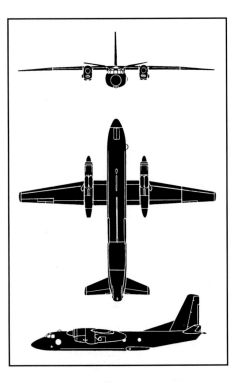

Nation: Ukraine
First flown: 1959
Passenger capacity: 44–52
Cruising speed: 280 mi (448 km)/hr
Range: 1500 mi (2400 km)
Length: 77.1 ft (23.5 m)   **Wingspan:** 95.8 ft (29.2 m)
Versions: An-24, An-24V (50 passengers), An-24T and RT (freighters), An-26 (redesigned rear fuselage and new engines)
Look-alikes: An-24/26, *Fokker F27/F50,* and *Let L 410/ L 420* are the only airliners in this subgroup with tailplanes which slope upward from the fuselage. To discern these from one another: *Fokker F27/50* has a more pointed nose than An-24/An-26, and *Let L 410/ L 420* tailfin extends below the aft fuselage.

Designed as short-haul feeder planes for Aeroflot, over 1000 of these types have been built. While Aeroflot operates by far the largest number, the An-24 and An-26 have also been extensively exported to former Soviet allies and client states in Europe, Africa, and Asia, as well as to Cuba. The An-24 is still being produced in the People's Republic of China, where it is known as the Y7-100. *Specs:* An-24; *Silhouette:* An-26; *Photo:* An-24.

CASA C-212 Aviocar

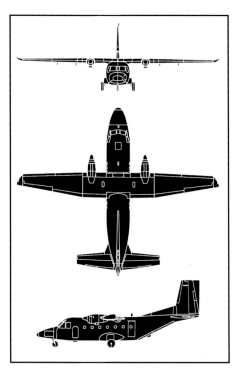

Nation: Spain
First flown: 1971
Passenger capacity: 26
Cruising speed: 228 mi (365 km)/hr
Range: 260 mi (410 km)
Length: 49.9 ft (15.2 m)　　**Wingspan:** 62.3 ft (19.0 m)
Versions: Series 200 (more powerful engines and higher operating weight), Series 300 (new engines, addition of winglets extending upward from the ends of the wings)
Look-alikes: Aviocar, *Aérospatiale N 262, Airtech CN-235, Dornier 228, Let L 410/L 420* and *Shorts 360* are distinguished by landing gear pods of various shapes and sizes protruding from the lower part of their fuselages under the wings. To discern these from one another: *Dornier 228* has a more pointed nose than Aviocar, while *Aérospatiale N 262* and *Airtech CN-235* have less pointed noses than Aviocar; *Shorts 360* has braces extending from the landing gear pods on the fuselage upward to the wings on either side; and *Let L 410/L 420* tailfin extends below the aft fuselage.

Originally developed for the Spanish Air Force as a replacement for its aging DC–3s and Junkers Ju 52s, the Aviocar has become popular in third world countries as both a cargo and passenger hauler. About 500 have been built on production lines which have been set up both in Spain and Indonesia. *Specs:* Series 200; *Silhouette:* Series 300; *Photo:* Series 200.

de Havilland DHC-6 Twin Otter

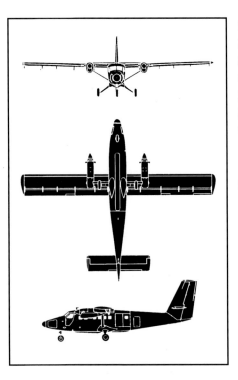

Nation: Canada
First flown: 1965
Passenger capacity: 20
Cruising speed: 210 mi (336 km)/hr
Range: 1110 mi (1780 km)
Length: 51.8 ft (15.8 m)   **Wingspan:** 64.9 ft (19.8 m)
Versions: Series 100 (original), Series 200 (extended nose), Series 300 (externally identical to 200 with upgraded engines)

Look-alikes: The absence of landing gear pods which protrude from the lower part of the fuselage under the wings distinguish Twin Otter, *Antonov An24/An-26,* and *Fokker F27/F50* from other planes in this subgroup. Tailfins extending further forward on the fuselage distinguish *Antonov An24/An-26* and *Fokker F27/F50* from Twin Otter, whose other definitive features are small size, non-retractable landing gear, and pointed nose.

A ble to operate from short, rough runways, the Twin Otter has been sold to airlines in more than 70 nations. It is also flown by the armed forces of Canada (CC–138) and the U.S. (UV–18). A floatplane variant differs in having a shortened nose and additional fins above and below the tailplanes. Over 800 of this highly successful and versatile airplane have been built. *Specs:* Series 300; *Silhouette:* Series 200; *Photo:* Series 300.

Dornier 228

Nation: Germany
First flown: 1981
Passenger capacity: 15−19
Cruising speed: 266 mi (427 km)/hr
Range: 1080 mi (1728 km)
Length: 54.4 ft (16.6 m)   **Wingspan:** 55.8 ft (17.0 m)
Versions: Do 228-100, 228-200 (stretched fuselage), 228-201 (reinforced structure/landing gear), 228-212 (current production model).

Look-alikes: Dornier 228, *Aérospatiale N 262, Airtech CN-235, CASA C-212 Aviocar, Let L 410/L 420* and *Shorts 360* are distinguished by landing gear pods of various shapes and sizes protruding from the lower part of their fuselages under the wings. To discern these from one another: Dornier 228 has a more pointed nose than *Aérospatiale N 262, Airtech CN-235,* and *CASA C-212 Aviocar; Shorts 360* has braces extending from the landing gear pods on the fuselage upward to the wings on either side; and *Let L 410/L 420* tailfin extends below the aft fuselage.

The Dornier 228 design features a uniquely shaped high technology wing and incorporation of composite materials into the fuselage and wing structures. The model -200 is 11 feet (3.4 m) longer than the -100 and can accommodate four more passengers; however, with shortened range. The current -212 model includes improvements which enhance operation from short runways, and improved avionics. Almost 300 of all versions have been produced. *Specs:* -200; *Silhouette:* -200; *Photo:* -200.

Fokker F27/F50

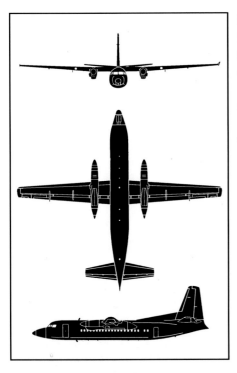

Nation: Netherlands

First flown: *F27* 1955; *F50* 1985

Passenger capacity: *F27* 28−60; *F50* 50−58

Cruising speed: *F27* 298 mi (477 km)/hr
F50 324 mi (518 km)/hr

Range: *F27* 1380 mi (2210 km); *F50* 1860 mi (2980 km)

Length: *F50* 82.7 ft (25.2 m)   **Wingspan:** 95.1 ft (29.0 m)

Versions: F27, Mk 200/F27A (improved engines), Mk500 (stretched by 4.9 ft [1.5 m]), F50-100 (virtually identical in external appearance to F27 with updated engines and technology), F50-200 (improved engines)

Look-alikes: The absence of landing gear pods distinguish F27/F50, *de Havilland DHC-6 Twin Otter,* and *Antonov An24/An-26* from other planes in this subgroup. *De Havilland DHC-6 Twin Otter* tailfin extends much less further forward on the fuselage than on F27/F50, while F27/F50 have a more pointed nose than *Antonov An-24/An-26.*

Almost 800 F27s were built before being replaced by the F50 in 1985; to date, almost 200 F50s have been produced. Both F27 and F50 are flown by many airlines and may be observed worldwide as short-haul connectors for both passengers and freight. Of all the airliners touted as DC-3 replacements, these models arguably come closest in function and general acceptance to fulfilling the role. *Silhouette:* F50; *Photo:* F27.

Let L 410/L 420

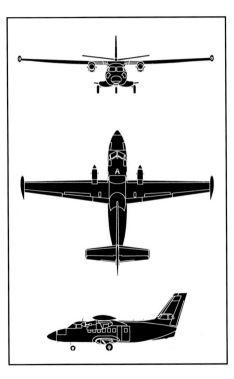

Nation: Czech Republic
First flown: *L 410* 1969; *L 420* 1993
Passenger capacity: 19
Cruising speed: *L 410* 175 mi (280 km)/hr
　　　　　　　　L 420 244 mi (390 km)/hr
Range: *L 410* 820 mi (1320 km)
　　　　L 420 850 mi (1370 km)
Length: 47.3 ft (14.4 m)　**Wingspan:** 65.6 ft (20.0 m)
Versions: L 410, L 410 UVP (1.5 ft [0.5 m] stretch, improved engines), L 420 (improved engines resulting in higher capacity)
Look-alikes: Let L 410/L 420 tailfin extends below the aft fuselage, distinguishing them from other airliners in this subgroup.

Built originally to fulfill Soviet requirements for a 15-seat short range airliner able to operate from rough fields, the L 410 has evolved into the L 420, which is aimed at cracking the lucrative western market. Over 1000 L 410s have been produced, most of which have been delivered to Aeroflot. Externally the L 410 and L 420 are almost identical. *Silhouette:* L 410; *Photo:* L 410.

Shorts 360

Nation: United Kingdom
First flown: 1981
Passenger capacity: 36
Cruising speed: 249 mi (398 km)/hr
Range: 1000 mi (1600 km)
Length: 70.5 ft (21.5 m)   **Wingspan:** 74.8 ft (22.8 m)
Versions: 360, 360-300 (improved engines and cabin), 360-300F (freighter)
Look-alikes: Shorts 360 and the *de Havilland DHC-6 Twin Otter* are the only airliners in this subgroup with braces extending from the fuselage up to the wings on either side. The braces on the *de Havilland DHC-6 Twin Otter* attach to the engines on the wing, whereas Short 360's braces connect directly to the wing.

The Shorts 360 is an updated design of the Shorts 330 with an enlarged fuselage, a new tail, and improved engines. Changes made in U.S. airline regulations in 1978 allowed Shorts and other aircraft companies to design commuter planes larger than the previous 30-seat capacity. *Specs:* 360–300; *Silhouette:* 360; *Photo:* 360–300.

Avions de Transport Régional ATR 42/ATR 72

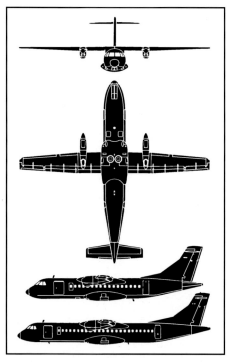

Nations: Italy, France

First flown: *ATR 42* 1984; *ATR 72* 1985

Passenger capacity: *ATR 42* 42–50; *ATR 72* 64–74

Cruising speed: *ATR 42* 308 mi (493 km)/hr
ATR 72 329 mi (526 km)/hr

Range: *ATR 42* 1209 mi (1934 km)
ATR 72 1666 mi (2666 km)

Length: *ATR 42* 74.5 ft (22.7 m)   **Wingspan:** 80.7 ft (24.6 m)

Versions: ATR 42-300 (original version), ATR 42F (freighter), ATR 42-500 (improved airframe, interior and engines, longer range), ATR 72 (stretch by 14.8 ft [4.5 m]), ATR 72-210 (improved engines)

Look-alikes: ATR 42/ATR 72 have landing gear pods protruding from the lower fuselage under the wings, absent on *de Havilland DHC-8 Dash 8*. *Let L 610* has a more pointed nose than ATR 42/72. ATR 42/ATR 72 tailfin extends forward on the fuselage, a feature absent on *Dornier 328*.

Jointly developed by Aérospatiale of France and Aeritalia of Italy, these successful regional airliners are flown worldwide. Over 300 ATR 42s and about 175 ATR 72s have been sold. *Main silhouette:* ATR 42; *Lower side view silhouette:* ATR 72; *Photo:* ATR 42.

de Havilland DHC-8 Dash 8

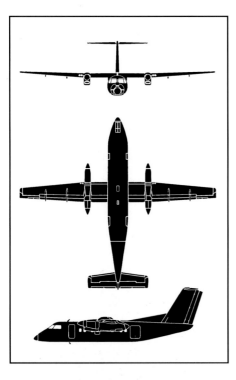

Nation: Canada
First flown: 1983
Passenger capacity: 36−56
Cruising speed: 346 mi (554 km)/hr
Range: 1250 mi (2000 km)
Length: 73.1 ft (22.3 m)   **Wingspan:** 85.0 ft (25.9 m)
Versions: Series 100, Series 200 (improved engines) Series 300 (stretched fuselage)
Look-alikes: *Avions de Transport Régional ATR 42/ATR 72* have landing gear pods protruding from the lower fuselage under the wings, absent on Dash 8. *Dornier 328* has a less pointed nose, its fuselage extends further behind its tailfin, and its tailplanes extend from a point slightly lower on the tailfin than on Dash 8. *Let L 610* has a more pointed nose than Dash 8, and its tailplanes extend from a point somewhat lower on the tailfin than on Dash 8.

A scaled-down version of de Havilland's Dash 7, the Dash 8 is intended for commuter airline use. It has also been adapted by the military for use in versions including the Canadian Air Force CC-142 (passenger/cargo) and U.S. Air Force E-9A (surveillance/communications). Over 400 Dash 8s of all versions have been produced. *Specs:* Series 100; *Silhouette:* Series 100; *Photo:* Series 100.

Dornier 328

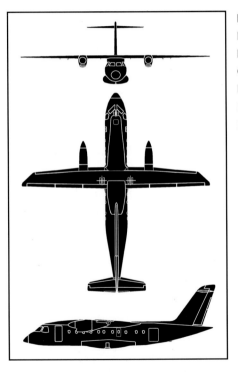

Nation: Germany
First flown: 1991
Passenger capacity: 33
Cruising speed: 388 mi (620 km)/hr
Range: 970 mi (1560 km)
Length: 69.6 ft (21.2 m)   **Wingspan:** 68.8 ft (21.0 m)
Look-alikes: *Avions de Transport Régional ATR 42/ATR 72* tailfin extends forward on the fuselage, a feature absent on Dornier 328. Dornier 328 has a less pointed nose and its fuselage extends further behind its tailfin than on *de Havilland DHC-8 Dash 8* or *Let L 610*.

The Dornier 328 is a technologically advanced short-range airliner. With a wing based on the successful design of the Dornier 228, the 328 boasts significantly higher speed and increased capacity. A considerable portion of its airframe is produced in countries outside of Germany, including Israel, the United Kingdom, Korea, and Italy.

Let L 610

Nation: Czech Republic
First flown: 1988
Passenger capacity: 40
Cruising speed: 299 mi (478 km)/hr
Range: 1580 mi (2530 km)
Length: 70.2 ft (21.4 m)   **Wingspan:** 84.0 ft (25.6 m)
Look-alikes: L 610 has a more pointed nose and tailplanes extend from a point somewhat lower on the tailfin than *de Havilland DHC-8 Dash 8*. L 610 has a more pointed nose than *Avions de Transport Régional ATR 42/ATR 72*. *Dornier 328* has a less pointed nose and its fuselage extends further behind its tailfin than on L 610.

An extended fuselage derivative of the Let L 410, the L 610 was originally designed in the mid–1980s as a 40-seat regional airliner for Aeroflot. However, with the breakup of the Soviet Union sales to Aeroflot flagged and attempts were made to export a new version, the 610G, equipped with western engines and avionics. A few L 610s are in service with Aeroflot, as well as in Europe, South America, and India.

Shorts 330

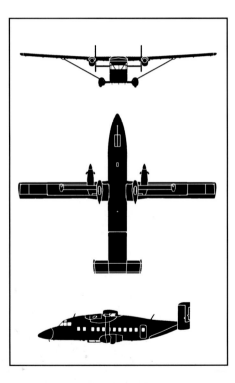

Nation: United Kingdom
First flown: 1974
Passenger capacity: 30
Cruising speed: 220 mi (352 km)/hr
Range: 1060 mi (1700 km)
Length: 58.1 ft (17.7 m)   **Wingspan:** 74.8 ft (22.8 m)
Versions: –100 (original model), –200 (improved engines), 330-UTT (military transport), Sherpa (freighter with rear door)
Look-alikes: The extended fuselage of Shorts 330 makes it easy to discern from *Shorts Skyvan,* which has a considerably shorter and differently shaped fuselage.

The Shorts 330, an evolution of the Shorts Skyvan, was intended as an inexpensive 30-seat commuter transport. Over 100 have been sold. The plane is in service with the U.S. Air Force in its Sherpa freighter version as the C–23A.

Shorts Skyvan

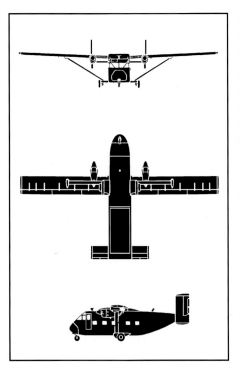

Nation: United Kingdom
First flown: 1963
Passenger capacity: 19
Freight capacity: 4641 lb (2100 kg)
Cruising speed: 200 mi (320 km)/hr
Range: 690 mi (1110 km)
Length: 40.0 ft (12.2 m)   **Wingspan:** 64.9 ft (19.8 m)
Versions: Skyvan, Skyvan Series 2 and Series 3 (updated engines), Skyliner (improved interior for passenger comfort)
Look-alikes: The foreshortened fuselage of Shorts Skyvan makes it easy to discern from the considerably longer fuselage of the *Shorts 330*.

A lthough adapted to commuter transport, the Skyvan's original incarnation was as a light freighter. In its cargo-carrying configuration, loading proceeds through an underside rear door. A rugged aircraft with good performance from short runways, a total of 150 had been built when production ceased in 1987. *Silhouette:* Series 3; *Photo:* Series 3.

Airliner Observation Log

Airliner	Date	Airline	Airport
Aérospatiale N 262			
Airbus A300			
Airbus A310			
Airbus A320			
Airbus A330			
Airbus A340			
Airtech CN-235			
Antonov An-12			
Antonov An-24/An-26			
Antonov An-124			
Antonov An-225			
ATR 42/ATR72			
Avro RJ/British Aerospace 146			
Beechcraft 1900C			

Airliner	Date	Airline	Airport
Boeing 707			
Boeing 727			
Boeing 737			
Boeing 747			
Boeing 757			
Boeing 767			
Boeing 777			
BAe 748/ATP/Jetstream 61			
BAe One-Eleven			
BAe/Aérospatiale Concorde			
Canadair Challenger/Regional Jet			
CASA C-212 Aviocar			
Convair 240-640			
de Havilland DHC-6 Twin Otter			
de Havilland DHC-7 Dash 7			
de Havilland DHC-8 Dash 8			

Airliner	Date	Airline	Airport
Dornier 228			
Dornier 328			
Douglas DC-3			
Douglas DC-4			
Douglas DC-6/DC-7			
Embraer EMB-110 Bandeirante			
Embraer EMB-120 Brasilia			
Embraer EMB-145			
Fairchild Metro			
Fokker F27/F50			
Fokker F28/F70/F100			
Gulfstream I/I-C			
Gulfstream II/III/IV			
Ilyushin IL-62			
Ilyushin IL-86/IL-96			
Ilyushin IL-114			

Airliner	Date	Airline	Airport
Jetstream 31/41			
Let L 410/L 420			
Let L 610			
Lockheed C-5 Galaxy			
Lockheed C-130/L-188			
Lockheed L-1011 TriStar			
Lockheed L-188 Electra			
McDonnell Douglas DC-8			
McDonnell Douglas DC-10/MD-11			
McDonnell Douglas DC-9/MD-80/MD-90			
Saab 340/Saab 2000			
Shorts 330			
Shorts 360			
Shorts Skyvan			
Tupolev Tu-134			
Tupolev Tu-154			

Airliner	*Date*	*Airline*	*Airport*
Tupolev Tu-204			
Vickers Viscount			
Yakovlev Yak-40			
Yakovlev Yak-42			

Index

Photo Credits

Front cover ... *American Airlines*
Title page ..... *Airbus*
Page 13 .... *British Aerospace*
Page 17 .... *Airbus*
Page 19 .... *Buffalo Airways*
Page 21 .... *Northwest Airlines*
Page 23 .... *Ilyushin*
Page 25 .... *Southern Air Transport*
Page 27 .... *Antonov*
Page 29 .... *British Aerospace*
Page 31 .... *United States Air Force*
Page 33 .... *Warren Disbrow*
Page 37 .... *Airbus*
Page 39 .... *Singapore Airlines*
Page 41 .... *Airbus*
Page 43 .... *Airbus*
Page 45 .... *Southwest Airlines*
Page 47 .... *British Airways*
Page 49 .... *Polish Lot Airlines*
Page 51 .... *United Airlines*
Page 53 .... *Charles V. Robbins*
Page 55 .... *Delta Air Lines*
Page 57 .... *Federal Express*
Page 61 .... *Jay Selman*
Page 63 .... *Comair*

Page 65 .... *Embraer*
Page 67 .... *American Airlines*
Page 69 .... *Gulfstream*
Page 71 .... *Crossair*
Page 73 .... *Lithuanian Airlines*
Page 75 .... *First Air*
Page 77 .... *Allen Howell*
Page 79 .... *Yakovlev*
Page 81 .... *Yakovlev*
Page 83 .... *CSA Czechoslovak Airlines*
Page 87 .... *Air North*
Page 89 .... *Northern Air Cargo*
Page 91 .... *Reeve Aleutian*
Page 93 .... *British World Airlines*
Page 95 .... *Antonov*
Page 97 .... *Bombardier Regional Aircraft*
Page 99 .... *Lockheed*
Page 103 .... *First Air*
Page 105 .... *Zantop*
Page 107 .... *Otis Spunkmeyer*
Page 109 .... *Embraer*
Page 111 .... *Gulfstream*
Page 113 .... *Ilyushin*

Page 115 .... *Crossair*
Page 117 .... *Comair*
Page 119 .... *Air Atlantic*
Page 121 .... *United Express*
Page 123 .... *Comair*
Page 127 .... *Clinton H. Groves*
Page 129 .... *CASA*
Page 131 .... *Antonov*
Page 133 .... *CASA*
Page 135 .... *Bombardier Regional Aircraft*
Page 137 .... *Dornier*
Page 139 .... *Fokker*
Page 141 .... *Martin Novak*
Page 143 .... *Short Brothers*
Page 145 .... *TWA Express*
Page 147 .... *Air Ontario*
Page 149 .... *Dornier*
Page 151 .... *Jay Selman*
Page 153 .... *Short Brothers*
Page 155 .... *Short Brothers*
Back cover
  left .... *Continental Airlines*
Back cover
  right .... *Northwest Airlines*

If you enjoyed *Guide to Airport Airplanes,*

THE AIRPORT AIRPLANE COLORING BOOK

Illustrated by Richard King

Travelers and airliner buffs can bring the romance of the airport home or have their airport experience enhanced by *The Airport Airplane Coloring Book.* It includes airliners often observed at major airports, such as the Boeing 727, 737, and 747; the McDonnell Douglas DC-9 and DC-10; and the Airbus A300.

8 ¹/₂" by 11", 44 pages

$5.95 (without crayons) ISBN 1-882663-05-5
$6.95 (8 crayons included) ISBN 1-882663-04-7

THE VINTAGE AIRPLANE COLORING BOOK

Illustrated by Richard King

Bringing back to life the early barnstorming days of seat-of-the-pants flying, *The Vintage Airplane Coloring Book* engages and teaches children about the early days of flight. Among the planes depicted are the original Wright Flyer flown at Kitty Hawk in 1903, Lilienthal's biplane glider, and the infamous Gee Bee. Illustrator Dick King has flown several of the types in this book.

8 ¹/₂" by 11", 44 pages

$5.95 (without crayons) ISBN 1-882663-07-1
$6.95 (8 crayons included) ISBN 1-882663-06-3

Call (800) 350-1007 to order or to obtain our free catalog of aviation books & gifts

you'll also enjoy these Plymouth Press books…

FAMOUS AIRLINERS

by William F. Mellberg

Bill Mellberg chronicles the development of the modern airliner in words and with the aid of a large number of splendid pictures. Beginning with the Boeing Model 80, whose 12 passengers flew at a little over 100 mph and were the first to enjoy the attention of specially trained nurses called "stewardesses," *Famous Airliners* finishes with the Concorde, which carries 100 passengers at over twice the speed of sound and across the Atlantic in three hours. Covering more than 40 airliners, it includes over 70 stunning photos of vintage and modern aircraft.
6" by 9"; 162 pages; 78 photos; paperback   **$14.95**   ISBN 1-882663-02-0

THE SECOND WORLD WAR AIRPLANE COLORING BOOK

Illustrated by Richard King

History buffs, warplane enthusiasts, and connoisseurs of aviation art will appreciate *The Second World War Airplane Coloring Book*. It includes in-action renderings of such famous planes as the Boeing B-17 Flying Fortress, Supermarine Spitfire, Mitsubishi Zero, and Lockheed P-38 Lightning.
8½" by 11", 44 pages
$5.95 (without crayons) ISBN 1-882663-09-8
$6.95 (8 crayons included) ISBN 1-882663-08-X

Call (800) 350-1007 to order or to obtain our free catalog of aviation books & gifts

Guide to Airport Airplanes

Order form

Please send me:

_____ copies of *Guide to Airport Airplanes,* 2nd edition   *Each* \$14.95 _____

Michigan residents add 6% sales tax _____

Vermont residents add 5% sales tax _____

Ship to:

Total _____

_____
Name

_____
Address

_____
City/State/Zip

Checks payable to: Plymouth Press

Enclose order form with payment and send to:
Plymouth Press
42500 Five Mile Rd.
Plymouth, MI 48170   **Credit card orders:** MasterCard/Visa (800) 350-1007

Call (800) 350-1007 to order or to obtain our free catalog of aviation books and gifts

Table of Contents

Forces

You've worn headphones. You've watched TV. You've worked on a computer. Chances are you've also sat in a car. You may have even been on a high-speed roller coaster. The same force powers them all. That force is *electromagnetism*.

The word is a mouthful. But breaking it down makes it easier to understand. *Electro-* means "electric," as in electricity. *Magnetism* refers to the pull between certain metals. Electricity and magnetism were once thought to be two separate forces. But now we know they are both interrelated.

Electromagnetism

Jenna Winterberg

Consultant

Michael Patterson,
Principal Systems Engineer
Raytheon Company

Image Credits: Cover & p.1 YONHAP/epa/Corbis; p.7 (top) Art Directors & TRIP/Alamy; p.13 (bottom right) Lourens Smak/Alamy; p.25 (illustrations) Tim Bradley; p.6 Joseph-Siffred Duplessis; pp.25–26 Rob MacDougall/Getty Images; p.32 Lexa Hoang; pp.2–13 (background), 13 (center), 14–15 (background), 15 (bottom), 19 (right), 23–24 (background), 25 (background) iStock; p.9 (top) Scott Franklin and Miao Miao for NONDESIGNS; pp.14, 20 Courtney Patterson; p.21 NASA; pp.28–29 (illllustrations) J.J. Rudisill; p.20 Cordelia MolloyScience Source; p.16 (left) GIPhotoStock/Science Sources; p.18 Phil Degginger/Science Source; all other images from Shutterstock.

Library of Congress Cataloging-in-Publication Data

Winterberg, Jenna, author.
  Electromagnetism / Jenna Winterberg.
    pages cm
  Summary: "Electromagnetism - now that's a big word!
But what is it? For starters, it's the force that runs the
electronics in your home. Your TV, computers, and even
simple light bulbs use electromagnetism. You can't see
it, but it's hard at work. It may seem complex, but once
you break it down it's simple."—Provided by publisher.
  Audience: K to grade 3.
  Includes index.
  ISBN 978-1-4807-4645-9 (pbk.)
  ISBN 978-1-4807-5089-0 (ebook)
  1. Electromagnetism—Juvenile literature. I. Title.
  QC760.2.W56 2015
  537—dc23
                          2014034269